# HONOUR

# ON TRIAL

# HONOUR ON TRIAL

## The Shafia Murders and the Culture of Honour Killings

# Paul Schliesmann

Fitzhenry & Whiteside

10 9 8 7 6 5 4 3 2 1
Library and Archives Canada Cataloguing in Publication
Schliesmann, Paul
Honour on trial : the Shafia murders and the culture of honour killings
/ Paul Schliesmann.
ISBN 978-1-55455-278-8
1. Shafia, Mohammad--Trials, litigation, etc. 2. Shafia, Hamed--Trials,
litigation, etc. 3. Yahya, Tooba--Trials, litigation, etc. 4. Honor killings--
Ontario--Kingston--Case studies. 5. Trials (Murder)--Ontario--Kingston--
Case studies. 6. Murder--Ontario--Kingston--Case studies. 7. Afghan
Canadians--Case studies. I. Title.
HV6250.4.W65S35 2012        364.152'30971372        C2012-905568-9

Publisher Cataloging-in-Publication Data (U.S.)
Schliesmann, Paul.
Honour on trial : the Shafia murders and the culture of honour killings / Paul Schliesmann.
[  ] p. : ill. photos. ;  cm.
Summary: A study of the culture of honor killing based on the murders of three girls and a
woman who was passed off as their aunt, in what came to be known as the Shafia case.
ISBN: 9781554552788
1. Women – Crimes against. 2. Honor killings – Canada. I. Honor on trial. II . Title.
362.88082 dc23    HV6250.4.W65S3554 2012

Fitzhenry & Whiteside acknowledges with thanks the Canada Council for the Arts
and the Ontario Arts Council for their support of our publishing program.
We acknowledge the financial support of the Government of Canada through the
Canada Book Fund (CBF) for our publishing activities.

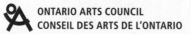

ONTARIO ARTS COUNCIL
CONSEIL DES ARTS DE L'ONTARIO

Canada Council     Conseil des Arts
for the Arts       du Canada

Design by Kerry Designs
All photographs used in this book were supplied as exhibits at trial,
with the exception of the photograph on Page 209
Printed in Canada by Friesens

MIX
Paper from
responsible sources
FSC® C016245

# Contents

RONA

ZAINAB

GEETI

SAHAR

# Introduction

FOR more than three years, as a reporter with the *Kingston Whig-Standard*, I covered the murders of Zainab, Sahar, and Geeti Shafia, and Rona Amir Mohammad.

The three-month trial that opened in Kingston on Oct. 19, 2011, attracted, for Kingston, unprecedented national and international media attention. Each day of the trial, TV network satellite trucks were lined up along the front lawn of the Frontenac County Court House, beaming their reports to the world. The media circus had come to town, bringing with it an urgency and intensity unfamiliar to the city.

The media is a ravenous beast and, in the Internet age, never sleeps. It was not unusual for me to start the day by giving a radio report from home, a telephone update for television somewhere along the road to the courthouse, then spend the morning listening to testimony, typing out a lunchtime hit for the Web, hearing more testimony in the afternoon, and then writing a 1,500-word story for the next day's edition.

The 12 men and women of the jury bore a heavy burden. The Crown did not have to establish the how and the where, nor even the why, to get a first-degree murder conviction. It was not necessary to prove which of the three accused dealt the final blow. The Crown had to prove only that they played a premeditated role in causing the deaths for all three to be found guilty.

Then there was the second court, that of popular opinion. Almost from the outset, the 150-seat courtroom was full every day until, by the end of the three months, people were lined up, waiting to get in to witness the morning and afternoon sittings. Every statement and piece of evidence was scrutinized. The foyer outside the courtroom was abuzz as Kingstonians mingled with journalists and discussed what they had heard, or speculated about what the next witness might reveal. While the sensational details of the case drew the public in, there was a real desire for justice to be served.

Throughout the trial, I was often asked how I dealt emotionally with the evidence. Forty-eight witnesses would appear over the course of the three months. With relentless news deadlines, there was little time for self-analysis. As journalists, we have to respect the legal process, particularly the presumption of innocence. We follow the story line like everyone else. What became most disturbing was watching the mountain of evidence pile up against the three accused as they sat stone-faced in the prisoners' box, showing little if any emotion, steadfastly denying responsibility for the deaths.

As the Crown played seemingly endless hours of interrogation videos with the accused, the performances were at times mesmerizing, almost dreamlike. Reality and unreality were often interwoven to produce a confusing narrative. In the absence of eyewitnesses, the three accused would tell police investigators and the court conflicting stories that defied logic. But in the end, the strange actions and contradictory statements of the accused proved their undoing.

We were all witnesses to a deeply sad story. But it was a story filtered through translations, video clips, and witnesses who expressed how little they actually knew about what was happening to the women in the Shafia household. With the murders, it became obvious that a new wave of immigration had brought with it challenges for young women wanting to fit into Canadian culture.

Since sitting down to write a book about the Kingston Mills murders and poring over the thousands of pages of evidence and transcripts, I've felt as if I were waking from some terrible dream. It was difficult at the time to believe that the three people meekly led into the courtroom each day in handcuffs, heads bowed and faces expressionless, could be capable of something as heinous as the crimes they were accused of. For all of us connected to this tragedy, the story of how these four women died will continue to haunt us.

Paul Schliesmann

# The drive home...

MONDAY, June 29, 2009, had been a warm 26°C in Niagara Falls, dropping a few degrees as evening approached. For a family about to embark on a seven-hour drive home to Montreal, 6:45 PM seemed like a late checkout time. The motel surveillance camera recorded it all, including the time. The young man paying the bill at the counter of the Days Inn in Niagara Falls was Hamed Shafia, conducting the transaction in English; his father, Mohammad Shafia, stood beside him, watching attentively.

The Afghan family of ten — three adults and seven children — was about to begin a long journey late into a southern Ontario summer evening. According to Mohammad Shafia, it was the decision of the whole family to leave so late in the day. They were travelling in two vehicles. Hamed and Mohammad were in the front seat of a silver Lexus SUV, Hamed at the wheel. In the back seat of the spacious luxury vehicle were two younger sisters and a younger brother.

The second vehicle was a black Nissan Sentra sedan. The mother, Tooba Mohammad Yahya, was the only licensed driver in the car. Beside her in the front passenger seat was her eldest daughter, Zainab. The 19-year-old was particularly anxious to return to Montreal. Zainab was about to become engaged to marry a distant cousin, a young man named Hussain Hyderi. She had spoken with him by phone that day and they planned on making their relationship official in just two days' time, on July 1. In the back seat of the Nissan sat two more of Tooba's daughters, Sahar, 17, Geeti, 13, and a woman named Rona Amir Mohammad, known to the Shafia children as "Mother Rona."

The 2005 Nissan had 113,130 km on it when Hamed and Mohammad had purchased it only the day before the family left on their vacation. A spacious Pontiac Montana minivan sat in the driveway of the family home at 8644 rue Bonnivet, in the Montreal suburb of St. Leonard. It was a tight fit for the passengers in the Nissan, especially for Rona, Sahar, and Geeti in the back seat. But no one cared. After the turmoil that had recently engulfed the family, the trip to Niagara Falls had come as a welcome and unexpected diversion, their worries left behind if only for a few days.

The Shafia family holiday had been an unusual excursion from the outset. A week earlier, on the morning of Tuesday, June 23, 2009, they'd headed north along Highway 117 toward the village of Grand-Remous on the Gatineau River. It wasn't their ultimate destination — far from it. The Shafias planned to drive all the way to Vancouver, covering a distance of about 5,000 km, remaining in Canada for the entire trip. That first day they travelled just 250 km to the town of Mont-Laurier and stayed there overnight. The next day the travel plans were suddenly and radically altered. The new destination would be Niagara Falls, the same vacation spot they had visited the previous year.

Before leaving Mont-Laurier, the family stopped at a McDonald's restaurant. Mohammad and Hamed went for a 15-minute walk. Father and son were close confidantes. Mohammad spent most of his time abroad on business trips, mainly in Dubai. He was a successful importer and had recently gotten into the lucrative business of exporting used cars to the Middle East. Hamed was getting more and more involved in the car business, conducting online car searches. He also helped manage the shopping plaza they'd bought in Montreal, collecting rent and arranging for work by tradespeople. At the beginning of June, Hamed had joined his father in Dubai, spending two weeks there. When they returned to Montreal, they informed the family of their plans for the cross-country trip.

Climbing back into the two vehicles at Mont-Laurier, the family now headed southwest, crossing into Ontario at Ottawa, then on to Brockville where they picked up Highway 401, the main autoroute across Ontario. By now it was evening and they were approaching Kingston, where they decided to take a bathroom break. The message travelled between the cars via Sahar's cellphone in the Nissan and Hamed's in the Lexus. The two vehicles turned off at the Highway 15 exit, took a right turn going north for a short distance, then turned left onto Kingston Mills Road.

They stopped at the Kingston Mills lockstation, the southern terminus of the historic Rideau Canal. The seven kids stretched their legs and wandered around the grounds as boats slowly made their way through the series of locks. They used the bathrooms located in the Anglin Centre next to the picturesque turning basin. Mohammad remained in the parking lot of the lockstation. The Shafias stayed for about a half hour to 45 minutes.

Mohammad Shafia and his son Hamed knew they would all be stopping here again in a few days on the return trip. What the four passengers in the Nissan did not know was that the trip and the car itself were part of a cold-blooded and shocking conspiracy.

# Kingston Mills...

THE morning of June 30 started out like any other for John Bruce, a canalman for 22 years with Parks Canada. His regular morning routine was to park his car at the lower level of the Kingston Mills lockstation, put his lunch in the office, and make his way to the upper lock area. His 11-hour shift began at 8:30 AM but Bruce usually got there around 8:00. There were a number of tasks to complete: raising the Canadian flag, taking the padlocks off the sluices that control water flow through the locks, putting up sunshade umbrellas, and marking water levels.

Routine is important along the Rideau Canal, which has operated continuously since its completion in 1832. Built by the British to enhance security against the sometimes-hostile American neighbours to the south, just across Lake Ontario, the Rideau Canal was never used much as the strategic military route it was meant to be. Hostilities between Canadians and Americans faded away and the railway eventually usurped steamboat travel. By the 1900s, the Rideau Canal had transformed from a commercial waterway into a popular vacation destination.

The two vessels John Bruce saw docked at the upper lock level on Colonel By Lake the morning of June 30, a houseboat and a sailboat, were typical of the canal's modern-day traffic. If these pleasure boaters wanted to be "locked through," they would have to wait. The normal routine at Kingston Mills was to move boats from the lower level first, lifting them from the waters of the Cataraqui River through the first flight of three locks, past the turning basin, then into the last lock that enters into Colonel By Lake, where Bruce was stationed.

There were, indeed, boats at the lower level this morning so staff began locking them through just after 8:30. Then Bruce made an unusual discovery – what appeared to be a car underwater and bumped up against the outside of the upper lock gate.

"I called on the radio once I realized there was a car, to tell them to stop," Bruce would testify in court just over two years later. "It was about 9 am. I saw oil rising out of the water. The car was right along the lock gate."

Along with the student canalmen working that day were two experienced Rideau staff members, Bob Martin and lockmaster Kevin Nontell. The lockages below were halted as Nontell and Martin made their way to Bruce's vantage point.

"We figured maybe it was a stolen car that had been dumped," Bruce recalled. "Kevin would have been calling the police. We stopped the locking operations." The car was in about 6.5 ft of lake water, its front end pointed toward the east wall.

For the lock staff, the fact that a car was impeding canal operations was more of a nuisance than anything. They'd seen a number of objects — including bicycles and even a snowmobile — dumped in the locks or the nearby millpond over the years. But when Nontell realized where the vehicle was situated — and the odd position it was in — it didn't seem to add up.

"It sounded so far-fetched, I thought it was a joke," the lockmaster would recall in court.

It wasn't just the position of the car in the water that was puzzling. How did it even get into the water where it was found?

"Nobody was thinking it was anything sinister. We were thinking it was a graduation prank — kids pushing a car into the water," Nontell testified on October 24, 2011, at the Kingston Mills murder trial. "It just seemed like a really odd place to find a car and probably not easy to get it in there. It would take some effort. It looked like something that would be planned."

At the scene, the police had not arrived after more than an hour, and Nontell made a second 911 call. Constable Brent White, a 10-year veteran of the Kingston Police force, received the dispatch at around 9:55 am. White was about a five-minute drive from Kingston Mills but, as he also noted at the trial, there was no real urgency to the situation.

At 10:23 am, White pulled up at the Mills where he was flagged down by John Bruce, who directed him through a green metal swing gate so he could drive his cruiser near the edge of the lock where the mystery vehicle had gone into the water. White and Bruce peered over the side.

"We get these calls a lot where you have a stolen vehicle in the water," the officer testified. He suspected some prankster had chosen this point of entry for a specific reason, thinking, "This is going to be found when the locks are opened the next day," he said.

Despite the feeling that he was dealing with an elaborate prank, White had several questions. "Is there a crime scene here?" he kept asking himself. After talking with John Bruce, White became even more suspicious. The gate through which he had just driven his cruiser was locked every night. Bruce was sure of that — it was part of his routine to check the padlock before leaving at 7:30 each evening.

A quick scan of the area indicated to White that the car would have had to take a winding S-shaped course around the lockstation grounds, past a substantial rock outcrop, to arrive where it had. "That gate was locked and wasn't opened up until the next morning," said White. "I'm thinking, How does that vehicle get there?'"

By 10 am, boat traffic had started to build at both ends of the lockstation. Lockmaster Nontell was relieved to see White show up. Lock staff were ordered to remain at the two-storey office located at the midway level of the operation. No work was getting done and the boats were backing up.

One of the boaters travelling northward up the canal that day, John Moore, asked canal staff what the delay was about. He was told that a car was nudged up against the top lock gate, so he went up to have a look for himself.

Moore turned out to be the right person at the right time at Kingston Mills. A lieutenant in the Canadian Navy, he'd been a ship's diver for 18 of his 28 years in the service. Along with his son and a friend, he had been camping at Cedar Island just off Kingston the night before. They were heading north to the village of Manotick. Moore had his diving gear on his boat so he offered to go down and assess the situation.

No one could give him official clearance to make the dive — not the Parks Canada staff, not Brent White. But Moore decided he would make the dive anyway and hefted his gear up the steep stone steps to the upper level of the lockstation. At the very least, he could get a licence plate number so police could run a check on the vehicle.

Around the time Moore was preparing his scuba gear, White decided to look around the lockstation grounds for some clues as to how the mystery car had ended up in the water. He found lacerations along the edge of the stone lock wall. "You could see where the concrete was scraped," he said.

This was puzzling in itself. The car had to be manoeuvred over the edge of the wall between the wooden steps of the lock gate and the metal winch — or "crab" — that staff hand-crank to open the heavy wooden gates to allow boats to pass through. This point of entry was only a few metres wide. It would have taken some tight turning to drive through that space in the dark. The car would have had to be moving at a fairly fast rate not to get hung up. On the top beam of the lock gate, White noticed two plastic letters — an "S" and an "E" — that would prove to be key pieces of evidence at the trial to follow.

White's tour produced more questions than answers. The upper lock at Kingston Mills is at the northern end of the station, cut off from the rest by Kingston Mills Road. Part of this section of road is a metal swing bridge that passes over the top lock. Canal staff turn this bridge when tall boats are being locked through. Otherwise, it remains in position as part of the roadway. From west to east along Kingston Mills Road sit the lock, the gate through which White had driven his cruiser, the rock outcrop, a section of curb, then the millpond controlling water flow over a series of rapids.

White walked around the rock outcrop and found faint black skid marks on the edge of the curb beside the roadway. Behind the outcrop, on the lawn, were two pieces of clear plastic, sitting in the moist grass. He picked them up for a closer look.

"[It] didn't really make any sense why they'd be there," he testified. "I took a look at them, made note of them, and set them back down."

A short while later, White led Kingston Police forensic identification officer Julia Moore to those pieces of plastic, thinking they might be significant. John Moore, meantime, had entered the frigid water. He swam toward the front end of the black sedan and noticed there was no licence plate. In Ontario, cars must have plates on the front and the back.

He made his way along the driver's side of the black car, noting "large, prominent dents and scrapes." Then he got to the driver's side window and found it rolled all the way down. He peered into the car and made a grisly discovery — a woman's body was floating in the murky water, her long, dark hair spreading out in ghostly tendrils. Then he saw a second body further in. The situation was suddenly — and drastically — altered. This was no prank. At the very least it was a scene of tragic misadventure, possibly worse. Moore swam to the back of the car, noted the Quebec licence plate number, and surfaced.

White had finished his tour of the grounds and walked back to the edge of the lock as Moore broke the surface. "I can remember him coming up and saying there's at least two females in there, maybe more," said White. "He gave me a licence plate number. They ran it through dispatch." White knew he had to act fast to seal off the area with police tape and call for assistance.

"I was thinking, this is pretty difficult, to get in this spot. [The car] would have to be driven in on purpose," he told the court. "This was either suicide or deliberate."

John Moore dove to the submerged vehicle a second time, this time noting more details. "I saw very clearly a young woman in the front half of the vehicle. She was not in a seat. She was floating."

Moore described the body as being in the "deadman's float" position. The Ontario Provincial Police diver who later videotaped

9

and officially noted the scene that day would identify the body as that of 13-year-old Geeti Shafia.

"I could tell she was very young," said Moore, who was shocked by the calm expression on the girl's face. "She looked like she might have just been having dinner, conducting normal day-to-day life and, suddenly, it was over."

He could see a second body behind Geeti's in the front seat. It was Zainab Shafia, also free floating.

Moore would offer up another observation during his time on the witness stand. The fact that the driver's side window was completely rolled down, he said, would have allowed "more than ample space for someone to get out of the vehicle. The driver's side window was fully open and she could have gotten out, even if she couldn't swim, and [stood] on top of the vehicle." The roof of the car was barely two feet below the surface.

There were no lockages on June 30, 2009, at Kingston Mills. The canal staff on duty, at least half of them summer students, were kept away from the upper lock and tasked to perform maintenance jobs like painting. The couple of boats that had started the ascent only made it to the middle lock, known to staff as the "fish lock," and were returned to the lower-level docks.

Information was sketchy. One of the staff had seen a car with a Quebec licence plate at the lockstation the previous day with several young women in it who appeared to be intoxicated. However, police were unable to establish any links between that information and what had actually happened.

# The night before...

IN the very early hours of June 30, about seven hours before canal staff made the chilling discovery at Kingston Mills, the phone rang in Robert Miller's bedroom. Miller was the manager of the Kingston East Motel and lived in the apartment behind the office, on call night and day. The man on the speaker phone asked Miller if he could book some rooms for the night. Miller checked the clock beside the phone. It was 2 AM. He asked the man to wait, got dressed, and unlocked the office door. Waiting for him were a short and stocky man in his fifties and a younger, taller, slim man with dark hair.

"They were both speaking and said they needed two rooms," recalled Miller. They wanted two rooms with two beds in each. The manager asked how many guests would be staying. There was a limit on the number of people allowed in each room. "The initial answer was six," Miller testified. "The younger gentleman said, 'There might be nine of us.' They sort of looked at each other and [then] said six. They settled on six people. I said, Will that be three for each room?' and they agreed." The two men conversed in a language Miller didn't recognize.

Rooms 18 and 19 at the Kingston East Motel each contained two queen-sized beds, a television, and mini-fridge. The younger man, Hamed Shafia, filled out the registration forms while his father, Mohammad, took the keys and went over to the rooms. Hamed paid in cash then left the office. Miller stood at the desk and filled in the registration book.

While he was still at the counter, Miller looked out the office window and saw the SUV the men had just arrived in backing away from the building. The only way in and out of the motel grounds was along the driveway running past the front office. Miller said he got a brief glimpse of the driver. It appeared to be the younger man. Miller thought this was strange. Barely 20 minutes had elapsed since the pair had first appeared at the office door.

Stranger still to Miller was the direction in which the SUV headed when it got out to Highway 15 — it went north toward Highway 401.

"It struck me as a little odd someone would come in at two in the morning and leave and go back toward the highway," he testified. A right turn would have taken them toward downtown Kingston and a Tim Hortons restaurant a couple of kilometres away from the motel that would be open at that hour.

His interest piqued, Miller decided to stay up for a while to see when the SUV returned. He played a video card game until deciding it was time to turn in. He had to be back on duty at 6 am. The last thing he did was check the time on his computer. It was 2:26 am and the vehicle still hadn't returned.

"I can see right down the line where the parking lot is," Miller told the court. "They would be driving back more or less in front of me." Why, he wondered, would two late-night travellers book two rooms for six people and then, why, almost immediately, would one of them drive off into the night again?

Miller and his wife were up at 5:45 that morning. He had a coffee and a cigarette before settling into the routine of the day. Motel guests began to check out and housekeeper Christine Bolarinho arrived to clean the rooms.

At about 8:30, Mohammad Shafia, the older man, appeared at the office asking to buy a $10 phone card so he could make a long-distance call. Shafia asked Miller if he could place the call for him from the office to a number with a 514 area code — the exchange for Montreal. Miller called but got a cellphone message and told Shafia there was no answer. He wrote on a piece of paper the directions for placing calls from the rooms.

Shortly afterward, Miller left to go into Kingston. When he got back, the housekeeper told him there was still no activity in rooms 18 and 19 and the 11 am checkout time was fast approaching. Miller went down to room 19. Mohammad Shafia came outside and asked if they could have the room for another half hour because their son was coming to pick them up. Miller looked into the room and saw a dark-haired woman, likely in her 40s, lying down facing the window, her head at the foot of the bed. He didn't see anyone else in the room.

The SUV the men had arrived in the night before was not in the parking lot. Miller was working on the playground equipment when he noticed a "van-type vehicle come to the motel and park in front of 18 and 19."

Throughout the morning, Christine Bolarinho noticed people peeking out through the curtains of room 19. Every time she went by she could see the face of Mohammad Shafia, who would quickly pull the curtains shut. Bolarinho said this behaviour was repeated at least half a dozen times. Finally, she knocked on the door and talked to the woman, asking if they needed towels or any other amenities. This was Tooba Mohammad Yahya.

"She replied, no, her son was sleeping. Possibly after he showered they would need towels."

Later, Bolarinho said she saw a teenaged boy come out of the other room, number 18, around the same time a minivan arrived in the parking lot. A young girl, described by the housekeeper as about eight years old, came out of room 19. Bolarhino smiled and spoke to her, but the mother told her to go back into the room.

"The next thing, I seen the van come into the lot," Bolarhino told the court. "The older gentleman and the boy driving the van went into the office." Bolarhino wandered into the office, too. They were arranging to take the rooms for a second night, but they wanted it at a cheaper price.

"To me they were trying to get a lower rate on the room — the older gentleman [was]. I thought maybe there was a mention of it twice."

Once again, Hamed filled out the motel forms. But this time it was his father who paid — again in cash. Shafia had, indeed, asked if there was a discount. Miller told him no, just the standard rate.

Bolarhino, who had been working at the Kingston East for three years, found the encounters with the Shafias different from those with most other guests. "It was like nobody made eye contact with myself. When they walked by, they were straight ahead, head down," she recalled. "I just found them, not odd, but not typical tourists I dealt with."

Miller was asked at the trial if he had seen anyone else staying in rooms 18 and 19 that day. Just one after the minivan arrived, he said. It was a young girl Miller thought to be about six years old. At some point on the morning of June 30, the van left the motel. Miller didn't see them go and he would not see the vehicle or the guests at the motel again, even though they'd rented the rooms for another night.

The next people occupying rooms 18 and 19 of the Kingston East Motel would be police forensics identification officers.

# The report...

BARBARA Webb was the receptionist on duty at the Kingston Police station on June 30, 2009, when three people walked into the spacious, modern foyer around 12:30 pm and approached her glassed-in work area. The two men came forward while the woman hung back in the lobby.

"They came to the front desk to make a missing person report," said Webb.

The younger man, Hamed, did the talking while his father Mohammad listened. "He told me that his two sisters were missing and they were in a Nissan."

Webb already knew about the situation being investigated at Kingston Mills. "As soon as they mentioned it," Webb said, "I asked them to take a seat. I knew [police] had found a vehicle underwater — a Nissan."

Webb asked the Shafias for more information. "The son said, actually, there were four people missing," recalled Webb. Hamed listed his three sisters and "a woman." The young man said something to his father in an undetermined language, "then he said it's his dad's cousin. She's about 50 years old." They told Webb they were staying at a motel on Highway 15 and that "they woke up this morning and the car was gone and the girls were gone."

At around the same time the Shafias arrived at police headquarters, Detective Constable Geoff Dempster was coming in to work. Dempster's scheduled shift was 2 pm to midnight, but he'd gotten a call around noon from Detective Guy Forbes, alerting him to the discovery of a car containing two bodies in the water at Kingston Mills. Dempster's superior officer, Chris Scott, told him to head out to the Mills to conduct interviews. Dempster was headed off by Barbara Webb who told him that Detective Brian Pete was in the foyer talking to three people believed to be connected with the underwater Nissan.

Dempster and Pete decided to bring the family to the victim-witness office where they would have more privacy. "I realized at that point we were going to be making a next of kin notification to them," recalled Dempster.

Hamed was speaking and translating for his parents. He told Dempster they were supposed to check out of the Kingston East Motel at 11 am but that his sisters and their 50-year-old "aunt" had disappeared. Hamed confirmed three digits on the Nissan licence plate.

"Hamed was telling me there were four people missing," said Dempster. The detective decided then he would have to break the bad news to the Shafias that their family members were likely dead. He arranged for a Persian-speaking interpreter to come to the station and translate.

The detective moved quickly to support the Shafias in their time of loss, arranging for volunteers from the victim referral service. The next step would also be difficult, but necessary: to question Mohammad, Hamed, and Tooba and gather as much information as possible about what had transpired over the previous day.

Dempster also learned from Hamed that they had dropped

off three other siblings at a Tim Hortons on Highway 15 while they came to make the missing persons report. Hamed and Tooba drove back to get them, returning to the police station just after 2 pm.

# Back at the scene...

OUT at Kingston Mills, events were moving rapidly. There was a hole in the usual Kingston Police line-up that day. Detective Mike Boyles, the sergeant in charge of the major crimes unit, was out of town on training. In an unusual turn of events, Chris Scott and the head of the detective division, Inspector Brian Begbie, both drove out to Kingston Mills. "That was so bizarre," Scott would later recall, "[that] a staff sergeant and inspector would both go out to a scene."

As Kingston Police would learn over the next two and a half years, however, there was nothing usual about the Kingston Mills murder case.

Scott and Detective Steve Koopman drove together to the scene at around 11:30 am. By this time the temperature had risen to a cool-but-comfortable 21-22°C with clear skies and a gentle breeze. Koopman had been working on a murder case but suggested to Begbie that he, too, could help with the field investigation at the Mills. Begbie initially said no, but relented. Koopman would prove to be indispensable to the case, eventually writing a 400-page report tracing the Shafias' cellphone use in the days leading up to the deaths.

Taking control of the scene, Chris Scott began widening the parameters of the investigation. He learned about the two boats that had been moored overnight at the upper dock of Kingston Mills. Both had left before police could question them, heading north to the lockstation at Lower Brewers Mills. Scott ordered the locks at both Kingston and Brewers shut down and dispatched two detectives to intercept the boats.

Unfortunately, those interviews proved unfruitful. Though the people on the sailboat and houseboat had been sleeping just metres away from where the car had gone into the water, they'd heard nothing unusual.

Scott and his team also began assessing the situation based on the information brought to the surface by John Moore. One body could mean that the occupant had lost control of the vehicle and had an unlucky accident. On the other hand, the Quebec licence plate on the black Nissan Sentra might point to bikers from Montreal coming down Highway 401 to dispose of some bodies.

As the body count in the submerged car increased, so did the perimeter that Scott ordered secured around the site. All potential crime scenes are contaminated to some degree. This was a very public place where boaters, tourists, and locals came all hours of the day and night to fish or picnic or watch the boats pass through.

Some of the potential evidence had already been shifted — most notably the plastic letters, S and E, picked up off the stone lock wall and placed by staff on the top of the lock gate. In hindsight, Kingston Police also realized that driving their cruisers through the green gate onto the grassy area next to the lock had been a mistake that could potentially have covered up tracks left in the damp lawn from the night before.

By noon, with the number of confirmed victims still at two, police at Kingston Mills were told that the Shafias had walked into the Kingston Police station and reported four family members and a Nissan Sentra missing. Police knew by then that the car was registered to the Shafias. But where were the other two missing people? The diver had only seen two bodies. Did they float off into the lake? Were they even in the car?

"That's when we started to key in: Where are they?" recalled Koopman.

Late in the afternoon of June 30, Ontario Provincial Police diver Glenn Newell confirmed the third and fourth bodies inside the car. Newell had been on a dive in the Orillia area when he got the call to assist Kingston Police. He arrived at the Mills at 4:10 in the afternoon, was briefed by city police at the scene, then set up a dive plan.

Newell's first request was to have canal staff fill the top lock. The submerged car was outside the lock, butted up against the massive wooden gate. Water was streaming into the lock. He needed it topped up to equalize the pressure on either side of the gate and slow the current passing around the car.

Newell also set up the communications system needed to videotape the underwater scene and allow him to talk through his dive mask, which was wired with a microphone. He suited up and went into the water, carrying the hand-held lens for the video system.

Visibility in Colonel By Lake was about 15 ft that day. Using the camera lens, Newell carefully documented the scene, approaching the car from above. Video images later played in court showed the rear passenger side of the car wedged against the lock gate. The video moves from the dent in the right-front hood and scrapes and a dent on the left-front bumper to the open driver's side front window.

Then a shadowy image of a person's head resting against the door post shows briefly, and Newell takes the camera to the back of the car. The rear left window is down about an inch; the rear left taillight is damaged; then the Quebec licence plate comes into view — 699 ZCD. Swimming back along the passenger side of the car, Newell thought he could see three or four bodies inside.

"They were all piled on top of each other, almost. It was very strange," he said, describing the eerie underwater tableau. "It was difficult to tell which person would have been driving the vehicle."

Newell offered the court the same observation made by navy diver John Moore: "Most cases when you have a window wide open, people are trying to get out. In this case, it didn't seem that was even an option."

The officer, a 24-year veteran with the OPP dive unit, noted that no objects inside the car — including cellphones and a blanket — had gotten outside, an indication that there wasn't much force created by the water entering the cabin of the vehicle. A blue stuffed teddy bear sat in the back window, still and cold and soaked through.

"It didn't sink at any rate of speed or force that would blow everything out of it," he said.

Newell estimated the rate at which the vehicle would have sunk. "When a car sinks, the front end is heaviest. It will sink nose first. Once the car hits the bottom, it slows down the speed [at] which the vehicle sinks," he said, estimating a time of about "a couple of minutes" for the Nissan to fully come to rest on the bottom.

On land, meanwhile, the route the car had followed to its final resting place was becoming even more puzzling for police investigators. They needed to determine right away if the green gate near where the car fell into the water could have been unlocked overnight.

"If that gate was open, it becomes plausible that [the] car had gone through there into the locks," Scott Chris said in an interview following the trial. If the car had entered through that gate, it would support the family's later claim that the four women had gone for a joyride and accidentally found their way into the water.

Police were already one step ahead. "That was addressed at the time," said Scott. "The lock staff were emphatic about [the gate] being locked."

Newell's dive would bring more troubling questions to the surface. For instance, the car was facing the direction from which it appeared to have entered the water. This was odd, said Newell. "The car was in first gear, but to be wedged the way it was, it should have been in reverse." In a Nissan with an automatic transmission, first gear is usually only used on steep or mountainous roads. As well, several times during his court testimony, Newell noted how difficult it was to tell from the positions of the four bodies who would have been driving. None of the women had been wearing seatbelts.

Ninety percent of the time on dive recoveries, he said, someone is situated "in the proximity of the driver's seat area." In this case, it appeared that 13-year-old Geeti was closest to the wheel.

Newell began the grim task of removing the bodies from the Nissan. First out was the body in the driver's side rear seat, that of 17-year-old Sahar. She was wearing a pair of tight jeans and a sleeveless top. In her pierced navel was a stud with two stones. Her fingernails were painted with purple nailpolish, her toenails with black. "This was the easiest person to access," said Newell. He gently lifted her body out through the door and brought it to the surface.

Next to come out was Rona, the "aunt," seated next to Sahar in the middle of the back seat, her feet resting on the floor. Rona was wearing a blue shirt. There were three pairs of earrings in her pierced ears, and six gold bangles hung from her wrists.

Removing the bodies from the front was more difficult. Geeti was closest to the driver's door but she and Zainab were intertwined, their legs between the bucket seats. Geeti's head was behind the seat headrest, against the doorpost facing into the back seat, and her right arm was around the headrest. Newell brought the little girl's body to the surface next. Underneath her brown shirt, Geeti wore a navel ring, like her older sister Sahar, whom she idolized.

Zainab came out last. Newell described her body as "kind of floating a little bit, which is unnatural for women." Her feet and hands were down as if preparing to touch bottom. Her fingernails were painted a light shade of blue. She wore her black cardigan backwards, buttons done up the back in the latest teenage chic trend. She had ten cents in her pocket.

# The interviews...

DETECTIVE Geoff Dempster's blond boyish good looks and laid-back demeanour must have been deceiving as he interviewed and videotaped the three Shafias — Mohammad, Tooba, and Hamed — one by one, on the afternoon of June 30. But the youthful-looking officer had already worked three years with Toronto police and ten in Kingston, eight of those years with the sexual assault unit and two with the cold case squad investigating unsolved murders.

Dempster was prepared to offer as much comfort and empathy as necessary. He assumed that before him were the grief-stricken members of a family looking for answers in the deaths of their daughters and the woman they identified as Mohammad Shafia's cousin.

Dempster's supervisor on the case, Chris Scott, would later call the detective's interviews in the first 24 hours "brilliant."

Dempster's trained ear immediately began to pick up discrepancies in what he was being told. Hamed referred to Rona, the deceased woman in the back of the Nissan, as his "aunt." Mohammad called her his "cousin."

The interview process for the parents was laboured. Tooba and Mohammad needed a translator in the room, a Kingston woman who spoke Farsi, a dialect of Persian, relaying Dempster's questions and giving him the answers back in English.

It was a painstakingly slow process, but Dempster persevered. By now, the three other children had been brought to the police station and were also being interviewed by two detectives from the child sex-crime unit, Sean Bambrick and Caroline Rice.

At 3:45 on the afternoon of June 30, Dempster began his interview with Mohammad Shafia by offering his condolences. "I'm very sorry about what has happened today, but to better come to an understanding of why it happened, it's important for us to learn as much as possible and, to learn as much as we can, we need to talk to you and your family."

In the video-taped interview, the two men faced each other over a small table. Shafia was calm, dressed in a black short-sleeved shirt, grey pants, and sandals. He was a short, dark man in his late fifties, balding, with wispy gray hair cut close to his head. He had heavy black eyebrows and deep lines carved in his face. He acknowledged Dempster's condolences without emotion. Then the detective asked Shafia to tell him as much as he could about what had happened, starting anywhere he wanted, and providing as much detail as he possibly could.

Shafia explained that they had taken the children on a vacation to Niagara Falls. He had just returned from an extended business trip about two weeks earlier. "My main base is Dubai," he told Dempster. "I am in Dubai most of the time." The children, according to Shafia, had wanted to go to Niagara Falls — the same place they'd visited the year before.

On the tape, Shafia did not look or sound like a man who had just lost three daughters in a fatal car accident. Was he in shock? The mention of his Dubai business affairs set him off on a tangent; he told Dempster how he planned to transfer his business dealings to Canada and how he had recently purchased a shopping plaza in the Montreal suburb of Laval. "I paid $2 million for it," Shafia told the detective.

Mohammad Shafia came across as a businessman through and through. In later court testimony, he told how he'd gone to work at a very young age in Kabul, the capital of Afghanistan, to earn money for the family after his father's death.

Afghanistan is a landlocked country located in the centre of Asia and bordered by Iran, Pakistan, Turkmenistan, Uzbekistan, Tajikistan and China. Home to an ancient culture, the country has seen Alexander the Great, Genghis Khan, the British, the Russians, and the Americans cross its borders in an attempt to control and modernize it.

A young Mohammad Shafia, living in Kabul, moved into electronics repairs. With seed money from an uncle, he turned his small shop into a multi-million-dollar import-export business by importing Panasonic radios and Peacock brand thermoses, shipped in from Japan. "It was only me," Shafia would tell the jury at his trial. "I had the monopoly on importing those."

From 1979 to 1989, a major war was waged between U.S.-backed mujahideen forces and the Soviet-backed Afghan government, in which over a million Afghans lost their lives. In the 1990s, a civil war led to the rise of the extremist Taliban government. Canadian troops were deployed to Afghanistan in 2001 after the 9/11 attacks on the U.S., their combat role drawing to a close in 2012.

Shafia thrived during the Soviet invasion of 1979 through to their withdrawal in 1989. In 1992, however, his business was interrupted when the mujahideen captured Kabul and Afghanistan erupted into civil war. The Shafias, with two young children, Zainab and Hamed, fled east to Pakistan, setting off a series of moves that would take them to Dubai, Australia and, eventually, Canada in 2007. Shafia always provided for his family, making business contacts in Japan and China. In Canada, he continued to be industrious and successful.

Shafia's interview with Dempster revealed more insights into family life. He said Zainab was engaged to be married. "It was not finalized," he told the officer through the translator. "But we like the connection and she liked it."

Then the questions went back to the vacation. Ten of them travelled to Niagara Falls — seven children and three adults — and they were in two vehicles. It was also established that he, Hamed, and Tooba were the only licensed drivers in the family. Shafia made a point of telling Dempster that Zainab and his other son also knew how to drive, "but they don't have the licence." This bit of information, seemingly out of context at the time, would become another critical piece of court evidence.

Dempster wanted to know how they came to be in Kingston. Mohammad gave an account of the trip from Niagara Falls that started late in the evening, a detour to see downtown Toronto and the CN Tower, back to Highway 401, and a stop at a McDonald's restaurant. He went into long explanations about the smallest details. At Kingston, Shafia recounted, Tooba got tired and they decided to find a motel. He paid $103 for each room. The four women later found dead in the car checked into room 18. Then Hamed went to Montreal.

"Last night?" Dempster asked. Shafia answered vaguely

that Hamed had work to do in Montreal, to "check the building or something."

Later in the day, Kingston Police would receive some startling information. Early that morning, just before the car had been discovered in the water, Hamed had reported an accident involving the family's Lexus SUV — not in Kingston, but in Montreal.

Around noon, the three Shafias, including Hamed, had come to the Kingston station in a Pontiac Montana minivan. With the Nissan discovered at the bottom of the Rideau Canal that morning, how many vehicles had the Shafias taken on their trip?

And what had Hamed been doing in Montreal when the family had arrived in Kingston so late the previous night? Police now had more questions than answers in an increasingly complicated case.

Dempster wanted to know who stayed in which room at the Kingston motel. Shafia said the women who died were in room 18, referring to them as "the people who are not now," as if they had been apparitions and not his own beautiful daughters who had recently been so full of life.

Dempster pressed Shafia on Hamed's late-night excursion. Shafia told him the family wanted to stay in Kingston for two or three nights "if the kids were happy."

This was one of many inconsistent accounts Mohammad, Tooba, and Hamed gave about the early hours of June 30 which would be scrutinized at trial. The Kingston East Motel, practically in the middle of nowhere, was certainly no tourist draw. And why would Hamed drive off into the night by himself in the vehicle that would hold the most people, leaving behind the newly purchased Nissan that barely held five?

Shafia turned to the events of earlier that morning when he

got up to find "the car is not there." He discovered that the four women were not in number 18, adjoining 19, after he "pushed and the door opened." (Court would later hear that the doors were self-closing and locked automatically.) The TV was on, he said, and there was some luggage and a Thermos for tea. But no daughters. No cousin.

Shafia said he phoned Sahar and Hamed, but his daughter didn't answer her cellphone. (In fact, the last recorded call on Sahar's phone was at 1:36 am on June 30.) He reached Hamed in Montreal at around 7:30 and told him the Nissan was gone and that he wanted his son to come back immediately to make a report to police.

According to Shafia, the last they saw of anyone from room 18 was when they were all checking into the Kingston East sometime after 2 am. Zainab had come to their room to ask for the keys to the Nissan to get their luggage out of the trunk. "They didn't return the key," he told Dempster.

At this point in the interview, the officer excused himself from the interview room. Shafia didn't realize it, but Dempster was conferring with his colleagues who were watching the interview in another room. He returned with some focused questions to clarify details. Was the car Hamed took to Montreal, in fact, a Lexus? Where did they go in Toronto? Where was the McDonalds they stopped at? How did they communicate between the two vehicles while driving? Who was driving which vehicle on the approach to Kingston?

This last question would become one of the most puzzling and frustrating to get the Shafias to answer — right down to the end of the ensuing trial.

Dempster left the room again. Shafia, who had just lost three teenaged daughters, sat with his head against his hand, sighed occasionally, and shuffled his feet while the Farsi interpreter watched silently from the corner.

Dempster re-entered the room. What did Shafia think happened last night?

"I don't know. I don't know what has happened," he replied. "I just woke up in the morning and didn't see them. That's it. I don't know anything else."

Several weeks later, while being monitored on a wiretap placed in his van, Shafia had some unsettling and ugly comments to make about his daughters' deaths. For now, however, he was calm and in control. At 5 pm, Dempster ended the interview.

# The Montreal
# accident...

MONTREAL police constable Nathalie Ledoux was working traffic patrol the morning of June 30 when she was dispatched to respond to a 911 call in the parking lot of a shopping centre in St. Leonard, a suburb of Montreal, just a few minutes' drive from the Shafia home on rue Bonnivet.

When Ledoux arrived at the shopping centre at 8:03 am — about the same time canalman John Bruce was arriving for work at Kingston Mills — Hamed Shafia was there with the Lexus. He told her he had driven the SUV into a yellow guardrail beside the Intermarche grocery store. The left headlight was smashed and, after taking measurements, the officer could see that the damage matched up with the height of the barrier. She noted debris from the plastic lens beneath it.

What the 15-year veteran of the city police force couldn't understand was why Hamed chose to park where he did. The lot was virtually empty at that time of the morning. He had his choice of parking spots closer to the storefront. The guardrail was around the side of the building, protecting a garbage shed.

"I found that quite [peculiar]. He could have taken an easier way," Ledoux later told the court through a French translator. "Why would he have put himself in a corner in a complicated manoeuvre?"

Ledoux recalled Hamed being "very calm" as he explained what happened. "The only thing he asked me was, Can I get my vehicle repaired immediately?'" Ledoux told him he could not if there was an outstanding insurance claim.

Later that day, Ledoux got a call at home telling her that the Lexus incident she'd investigated early that morning might be "linked to another kind of crime."

# Gathering evidence...

A S soon as Kingston Police learned about Hamed's accident in Montreal — on the same day he and his parents reported Rona, Zainab, Sahar, and Geeti missing — they knew they had to get to Montreal to see the Lexus. Detective Steve Koopman drove on July 1 to the Holiday Inn Express, where the Shafias were now staying courtesy of Kingston Police.

Koopman brought Mohammad Shafia back to police headquarters where they sat down at 11:09 am for another video-recorded interview. The interpreter who had helped with the previous interviews was also there. Koopman wanted Shafia's permission to go to Montreal to inspect the damage to the Lexus. But first, the officer had a few other matters to clear up, in particular, why Hamed had made the late-night trip to Montreal and returned in the minivan.

Through the interpreter, Shafia told him: "He went in order to go to work the next day. Meaning, if this incident hadn't happened, he would not have come [back]. Do you understand, miss? If this incident hadn't happened, I wouldn't have asked Hamed to come here. I would've called him a few days later and asked him to pick us up then."

When questioned later by Dempster, Hamed would say he went to Montreal because he forgot his laptop, and returned to Kingston in the minivan because the Lexus "takes more gas and fuel and stuff like that."

Koopman asked Shafia if he and Hamed had spoken the previous night about the Lexus and the minivan. Shafia said he didn't even think about the vehicles because of his family's grief. "They didn't eat so we went to eat at McDonald's. My wife was crying and [I tried to] comfort her, [saying]: 'Now it's happened. God's brought it. What are you doing? [If you] are crying, the other kids will start to cry, and we might lose them, too.' We talked about this and nothing else."

Koopman asked about any damage that he may have seen on the Lexus before Hamed took it to Montreal. "No, I didn't see anything because the car was in good shape when it left and came back," Shafia responded.

Then he recalled something. "Although in Niagara," Shafia said, "Zainab, with this black car [the Nissan]... I was outside [the car]... it hit [the Lexus] a little bit but it didn't get scratched... it didn't get scratched. Zainab was coming back, reverse coming." This was another reference to what would be a recurring theme about Zainab's always wanting to drive and sneaking the car keys to do so.

Koopman tried to determine exactly where the Lexus may have been hit by Zainab while driving the Nissan in Niagara Falls. Shafia's story shifted ever so slightly. "She was reversing. I wasn't inside the car. I was watching from upstairs," he said.

Later in the interview Shafia claimed that Zainab even asked her mother if she could drive the Nissan on the highway, an astonishing notion, considering that she had no driver's licence and had never taken a driving course.

Shafia's recollections continued to jump around. "Even until the hotel, the car was perfect," he told Koopman, referring to the Kingston East Motel where they would later take rooms. "When we got to the hotel... and settle, my wife parked the Nissan."

Why would he suddenly introduce this specific information about Tooba parking the Nissan? As police would allege in building their case, Tooba never drove the Nissan to the Kingston East Motel. In fact, the Nissan never got there at all. Nor did the four women who died that night.

Koopman still had to get Shafia's permission to view the Lexus without resorting to a search warrant. Shafia claimed that this was the first he'd heard of the Lexus's being damaged.

"So why this is important for us," Koopman explained, "is that it's coincidental that he has damage to the Lexus when there's obviously some damage to the Nissan, and we just need to make sure that they're not connected."

Koopman eventually obtained permission to go that day to see the Lexus, suggesting Shafia could first seek a lawyer's advice if he wanted to. Shafia said he had no need of an attorney. "What I want is to know if my family member has been killed, has gone in the water, has been strangled, has been drugged. What has happened? That's what I'd like to know. If [s]he has taken drugs, if [s]he has gone mad. This is not human [i.e., normal] behaviour," he told Koopman.

Shafia said he, too, would go to Montreal so he could get clothes for his family. "Check the house, check the car, check street, check anywhere and ... I will go with them [the police] or won't go. I just want to find out who killed my family. Did [s]he kill [her]self? Did individuals kill [them]? What happened? I don't know," said Shafia.

Later that day, police found the Lexus parked inside the lower-level garage of the residence. What they discovered would turn out to be extremely valuable to their case: 10 pieces of plastic inside and around the vehicle.

## Aerial photo of Crime Scene
Photo and labels by Ident Officer ANDERSON
October 17th, 2009

## Upper (north) Lock and Nissan point of entry into water
Photo by Collision Reconstructionist PRENT
September 25th, 2009

## Location of Kingston East Motel in relation to Highway 401 and Kingston Mills
### Aerial photo and labels by Ident Officer ANDERSON
#### October 17th, 2009

Hwy 401

Kingston East Motel

Hwy 15

Kingston Mills Road

Station Road

## Plastic debris at #1 marker
### Photo by Ident Officer MOORE
#### June 30th, 2009

## Washroom entrance at rear of "house" (south side)
Photo by Ident ANDERSON
September 4th, 2009

## Damage to rear driver's side – Nissan
Photo by Ident Officer MOORE
June 30th, 2009

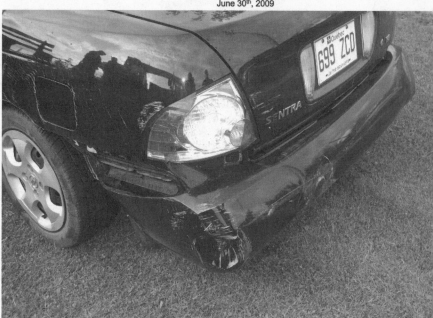

# Damage to Lexus driver's side headlight- Montreal
## Photo by Detective Constable KOOPMAN
### July 1st, 2009

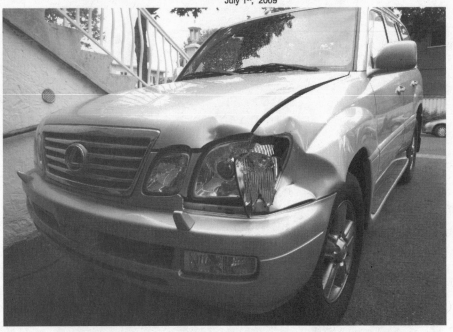

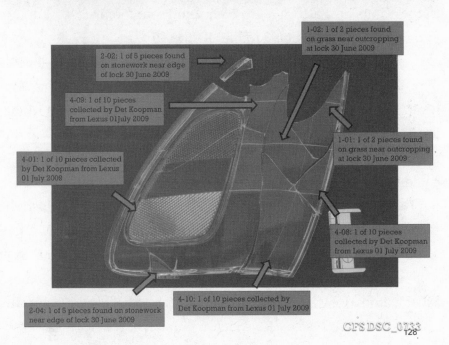

1-02: 1 of 2 pieces found on grass near outcropping at lock 30 June 2009

2-02: 1 of 5 pieces found on stonework near edge of lock 30 June 2009

4-09: 1 of 10 pieces collected by Det Koopman from Lexus 01July 2009

1-01: 1 of 2 pieces found on grass near outcropping at lock 30 June 2009

4-01: 1 of 10 pieces collected by Det Koopman from Lexus 01 July 2009

4-08: 1 of 10 pieces collected by Det Koopman from Lexus 01 July 2009

4-10: 1 of 10 pieces collected by Det Koopman from Lexus 01 July 2009

2-04: 1 of 5 pieces found on stonework near edge of lock 30 June 2009

# The pieces fit...

KINGSTON Police forensic identification officer Robert Ether
ington joined the Kingston Mills investigation on July 2 whe
he accompanied the bodies of the four women to Ottawa Genera
Hospital, where autopsies would be performed by the pathologis
Dr. Christopher Milroy. It was a long day for Etherington who wa
at the morgue in Kingston General Hospital at 6 AM to sign out th
bodies. The examinations, which he photographed, ended at 6 PM
He got back to Kingston just before 9 PM and was immediately ser
to the Kingston East Motel to complete more forensic work and t
photograph the contents of rooms 18 and 19.

On the morning of July 3, Etherington signed out the piece
of plastic retrieved two days earlier from the garage at 8644 rue Bor
nivet. Then he looked at Julia Moore's forensics photos from Kings
ton Mills, particularly the pieces of plastic found in the grass and a
the lock edge. It was a moment of revelation for Etherington. "Ther
could be an association between these pieces," he recalled in cour
In other words, if the pieces of plastic found at the lock matched th
pieces from Montreal, it would place the Lexus at Kingston Mills.

Etherington immediately contacted his boss, Inspector Bria
Begbie. "I advised him that these pieces appeared to fit together.
Etherington knew he was on to something. "I believed it was fairl
important, yes. These pieces shouldn't match to that turn signal ac

cording to the story we knew at the time," he said. "The vehicles were very important and obviously the scene was important, and something was going on we didn't know about yet."

The case was upgraded that day to a homicide investigation, though police didn't make that information public right away.

The plastic shards would be sent to the Centre of Forensic Science crime lab in Toronto, where it was determined that the pieces from Montreal and Kingston Mills were, indeed, "once part of the same vehicle."

# Growing suspicion...

"ONCE we had that physical evidence, we had concerns about the response from the family, such as [them] withholding information about the accident in Montreal," recalled lead investigator Chris Scott. "What's a typical response when you have four family members taken from you?" Clearly, not what police were hearing and seeing. There were also growing concerns for the surviving three children.

"We still had the [other] children in that family," said Scott. "You don't know the dynamics in the household."

Although police thought the Shafias' reactions were atypical, denial is not an uncommon response to the shock of losing a loved one to homicide. Nor are anger and rage. Although the anger is usually directed at the perpetrator of the murder, survivors can also be angry with the victim, for being in the wrong place at the wrong time, or for having a lifestyle that put them in danger. Feelings of guilt and intense anguish can sometimes last for years.[1]

According to Eric Schlosser, in his book A Grief Like No Other (1997): "In the days and weeks right after a murder the victim's family is often in a state of shock, feeling numb, sometimes unable to cry. The murder of a loved one seems almost impossible to comprehend. Life seems unreal, like a dream. Survivors may need to go over the details of the crime again and again, discussing them endlessly, as though trying to put together the pieces of a puzzle, struggling to make sense of it all."

Men may have difficulty grieving because they have been so-cialized to believe that real men should keep their feelings to themselves — expressing them is seen as a weakness. This would be even more likely in someone coming from a patriarchal culture like Afghanistan.

It's no wonder the police were confused by and even suspi-cious of the Shafias' responses. Nevertheless, the evidence, plus their gut reactions, were telling them something was not right.

Scott credits detectives Dempster and Koopman with con-ducting those early videotaped interviews with the Shafias.

"I thought it was brilliant in those first 24 hours — Detec-tive Dempster's interviews with Hamed when he asked, Were you there?' The physical response was telling. It wasn't like a shock. If you're being interviewed the day four family members were found and you were asked were you there, you'd be incensed," said Scott.

Koopman's interview with Mohammad Shafia on July 1 was all about obtaining consent so investigators could get to the Shafia home in Montreal quickly and without a warrant to examine the Lexus. Over and over again, he got Mohammad to say that it was fine for police to go to his home on rue Bonnivet. "I conducted the full video so the judge or jury could see he was fully aware of it," said Koopman.

Meanwhile, Kingston Police grappled with the puzzling ac-tions and statements of the Shafias.

Koopman had already begun to gather and analyse the cellphone data that would piece together the Shafia family's movements between June 23 and 30, from Montreal to Niagara Falls and back to Kingston.

1 http://www.cpomc.ca/survivor/homicide_survivors.shtml

The examination of those records revealed an aberration: on June 27, while the family was in the middle of their stay at Niagara Falls, Hamed's phone registered on the cellphone tower at West-brook, just west of Kingston. Police and the Crown concluded that Hamed and Mohammad must have travelled to Kingston Mills to more precisely plan the murders. At the ensuing trial, Mohammad Shafia claimed he was alone in the Lexus and heading to Montreal on business when his family called to say they were bored in Niagara and wanted him to return. Hamed's phone, he testified, just happened to be in the vehicle.

"They tried to make [out] that Shafia could have been in the vehicle with the phone. What's interesting is we had Hamed on video saying he always had his phone [with him]," said Scott. "He didn't even want to give it to his dad to go to Montreal on July 1," added Koopman. "It's weird a son is so attached to his phone he wouldn't give it to his dad in case of an emergency."

In his July 1 interview, Detective Steve Koopman asked Mohammad Shafia if there was any information he could release to the news media. Shafia asked for more time to notify family members, particularly Rona's people overseas.

"I was thinking about that," he told the officer. "I want to contact Rona's brother in France." As for his own family, Shafia said he had contacted some of them, but only to say in a general way that an accident had occurred. "I have to advise them slowly that one person has passed away, two people have passed away, but if all of a sudden I say four people have passed away, anyone would go crazy."

Many family members, however, did not wait to be contacted by Shafia about the deaths. Kingston Police had begun receiving disturbing information from friends and family of the Shafias living in Montreal and Europe. Their e-mail and phone calls insisted that there was much more to the case than originally thought.

Calls to police came in from Hussain Hyderi, the Montreal man engaged to Zainab. Fahima Vorgetts, a distant relative of Rona living in the U.S. — and one of her closest telephone confidantes over the previous year — knew Rona had been threatened by Mohammad and Tooba. Fazil Javid, Tooba's brother living in Sweden, and Latif Hyderi, Tooba's uncle in Montreal — Hussain's father — reported telephone conversations with Mohammad in which he expressed anger and outrage at his daughter Zainab's "shameful" behaviour.

"We are convinced this was a crime of honour, organized under the guidance of Mr. Shafia, his wife Tooba, and their oldest son, Hamed," wrote Rona's sister Diba Masoomi in a desperate e-mail from France.

The day of the homicide upgrade (July 3), Inspector Brian Begbie delegated assignments to his investigative team. He put Scott in charge.

As Kingston Police continued gathering evidence from the children's school and child-protection authorities, it would, indeed, point to this chilling motive — that the four murders were committed to regain family honour considered "lost" when the older girls developed relationships with young men.

"The investigation doesn't stop," recalled Scott. "Now we had the events from the time the Nissan is purchased to the girls' deaths. We had that cold. Now we're getting a picture of the family prior to this and that helps [us] understand motive and mindset."

# Shame and honour[2]...

WHY did the friends and family of Mohammad Shafia con-clude that the deaths of his three daughters and Rona were the result of an honour killing? The answer to that question goes back a long way, in fact, to a time of pre-religious, pagan Arab tribalism that has long since been incorporated into the culture and is now well established in countries throughout the Middle East and Asia, including India, Pakistan, Afghanistan, Jordan and Turkey, and the Balkans, among others.

In many of the families from these cultures, the "honour" of the entire family reposes in the female members because they are the bearers of children and, therefore, carriers of the lineage. The notion of honour, however, is also a reflection of male status. The man who is shamed by the women in his family through their "inappropriate" behaviour must act to restore his honour, most often by killing the offending woman. Inappropriate behaviour can be anything from the manner of dress, association with friends and boyfriends outside of the family and social group, defiance and disobedience, adultery, and even rape, and need only be suspected by male family members to prompt action.

Shame is a complex emotion that is connected to "face," and includes feelings of humiliation, embarrassment, and a sense of fail-

2 http://www.meforum.org/50/honor-murders-why-the-perps-get-off-easy
and http://www.japss.org/upload/19._Welden__opinion_paper_.pdf

ure. Men in a patriarchal society such Afghanistan's identify strongly with one another and are socialized to see themselves as superior to women. While men move freely in society, women are constrained. A family's honour requires that a man control the women in his family and any shameful act by one of them reflects directly onto him. If he fails to act, he will, in effect, lose his sense of social dignity and will be deemed by other men as weak.

The pressure on Mohammad Shafia and his son Hamed to restore the family's honour in the face of apparently shameful behaviour by some of the women in his family stemmed from a long and deeply embedded tradition, unquestioned by either of them.

# Rona's diary...

THE information coming to police from family and friends of the Shafias revealed another shocking piece of information: Rona Amir Mohammad, the woman found dead in the back seat of the Nissan, was really Shafia's first wife. She was not merely a cousin or an aunt but Shafia and Tooba's partner in a polygamous marriage. Rona and Shafia had become husband and wife in an elaborate wedding ceremony in Kabul in 1978.

The relationship was confirmed beyond any doubt on July 21 when police searched the Shafia home in Montreal. In a closet they found a diary Rona had kept for a short time in 2008. Handwritten in Persian, it described her deteriorating relations with Shafia and Tooba as well as her ostracism within the family.

The memoir was like a voice from the grave. It painted a bleak picture of Rona's life in the Shafia household. She talked about going on endless walks around the Montreal neighbourhood to fill her days and escape abuse and about how she was being isolated from the children she had helped raise. Known to the world as her husband's cousin in order to hide their polygamous marriage, Rona's temporary immigration visa was firmly under Tooba's control. Rona, by her own account, was a woman without social standing, friends, or citizenship.

Rue Bonnivet neighbour Mary-Ann Devantro recalled one

of the times several of the Shafia girls and Rona came to visit at her apartment. Believing Rona was, in fact, the children's aunt, Devantro asked why such a beautiful woman wasn't married. Maybe she would be some day, Rona replied wistfully, not daring to reveal the truth.

When Devantro commented on the delicately braided metal earrings Rona was wearing, Rona took them off and gave them to Devantro as a spontaneous gift. Today, they are Devantro's unhappy reminder of the beautiful woman with dark hair and sad eyes who suffered much and who, as it turned out, had ample reason to fear for her life.

The first entry in Rona's diary began with the Islamic incantation, "In the name of God, the Beneficent, the Merciful." Rona immediately launched into recollections of her early life in Kabul, about starting school at the age of five, and remembering her father, a retired Afghanistan army colonel. Rona had eight siblings — three step-sisters and two step-brothers from her father's first wife; and three sisters and a brother from the marriage between her father and her mother.

"We were a middle-class family. I had just finished 11th grade when my brother Noor married. Shirin Jan, who was a distant relative on my father's side, had come to my brother's wedding reception and saw me sitting there, quiet and subdued. She liked me and asked for my hand in marriage for her son from her first husband," Rona recalls.

That son was Mohammad Shafia, at the time a successful businessman growing his electronics sales and repair business in Kabul. Shirin Jan would visit Rona's home several times to get to know her prospective daughter-in-law. Rona definitely met with

51

her approval. Then Shirin Jan invited the girl and her family to he
home, Rona writes, "so that her son could have a good look at me
After our visit, her son announced his consent, so [they] stepped u
the khwastgari." This is the ritual undertaken by the groom's famil
for completing an arranged marriage.

"I knew nothing about such things," Rona writes, revealingl
"so when my elder brother came to ask me whether I accepted th
union, I said, 'Give me away in marriage if he is a good man; don'
if he is not.'"

The family checked Shafia out, reporting that he was, indeed
"a good man but not educated," his schooling cut short with his fa
ther's death. The engagement would go on for two years, until Shafi
and Rona were married in 1978 in Kabul's most opulent hotel, th
Intercontinental, with a grand feast and celebration.

"After getting married, my lot in life began a downwar
spiral, right up to today [while] I am writing these memoirs," Ron
writes in her diary.

Rona was unable to bear children. This was devastating new
for the couple so they spent the next seven years travelling back an
forth to India for fertility treatments. These were unsuccessful and
as a result, the relationship deteriorated.

"Finally, my husband started picking on me. He wouldn't al
low me [to] go to visit my mother, and at home he would find faul
with my cooking and serving meals, and he would find excuses to
harass me," Rona recounts. "I had to say, Go and take another wife
what can I do?'"

Rona offered to share her home with another wife so tha
Shafia could have children. He accepted this and insisted he woulc
continue to pay for fertility treatments. Then she learned that Shafi

had been quietly making arrangements with Tooba's brother-in-law for a second marriage.

The second wedding was also held at the Intercontinental. The photos of the day are unusual by Western standards: Mohammad, serious-looking in a dark suit, his hair and moustache thick and black, is flanked by his first wife on his left arm, and his new bride, Tooba, resplendent in a white gown, on his right. They look stiff and awkward on what should have been a day of celebration.

Just three months after this second marriage, Tooba discovered she was pregnant. They travelled to India where Zainab was born on September 9, 1989. Rona was treated once more for her infertility, but the doctor this time said Rona would need surgery to assist with pregnancy. But the family had to return to Afghanistan so the procedure was never performed. Just over a year after Zainab's birth, Hamed was born, on December 31, 1990, and Rona's importance in the household began to rapidly diminish.

Her position was further weakened by an unfortunate incident that took place shortly after Hamed was born. The family was lounging on the rooftop of their home. Rona was holding baby Hamed when she stood up and tripped. Both Rona and Hamed were injured, the baby requiring hospital treatment, some of it provided by Mohammad's brother, a doctor and medical professor in Kabul. Mohammad was livid, though Rona protested that it was an accident and she had been hurt, too.

"I suffered so much until his son got well again that I could not even think about my own condition," Rona writes. "[My husband] did not treat me and my family decently until Hamed was well again."

By this time, Tooba was pregnant with her third child, Sahar.

Despite Rona's bleak descriptions of her life in the polygamous arrangement, there was one bright spot. Out of the blue, Tooba offered to give the baby she was carrying to Rona to raise as her own. This is a custom in some Afghan households where one wife is unable to have children. Rona was delighted and took over the care of Sahar when the baby was just 40 days old.

They would be together 17 years later in the back seat of the Nissan Sentra at the bottom of the Rideau Canal — inseparable victims of a horrible crime.

# Nomadic life...

IN 1992, the Shafias fled Afghanistan and the conservative mujahideen regime that had taken Kabul during the civil war. With their three children and Rona in tow, Mohammad and Tooba crossed the border into Pakistan. They would stay there for the next four years.

According to Mohammad, he never felt his family was safe in Pakistan because of Pakistani support for the Taliban. By 1995, a repressive Taliban regime was in power in Kabul, and "liberal" people like his Afghan family were easy targets for persecution. Children were being kidnapped and held for ransom. Shafia was a wealthy man and had reason to fear such a thing.

They moved to Dubai in 1996, where Shafia's electronics business flourished. He became the top Panasonics dealer in the country, one time receiving a $50,000 bonus from the parent corporation. Shafia still held property and stocks in Afghanistan and the family remained prosperous — so much so that in 2008, after he had been in Canada for a year, he sold one of his two houses in Kabul for $900,000.

In 2000, he decided to try his fortune in New Zealand. The Shafias applied for visas but Rona's didn't clear for medical reasons. At the prompting of one of Shafia's business associates, they applied instead to Australia and were successful. What happened in Australia and why the Shafias left after a year is the subject of conflicting stories. Rona claims in her diary that the Australian government declared Shafia undesirable — that he hadn't created any wealth for Australians, only for himself, and that he disregarded the rules of his visa by purchasing property. At his trial, Shafia contended he was out of the country for much of the time on business trips and that Tooba was feeling isolated and alone in Australia. It was Tooba, he insisted, who pressed him to return to Dubai.

By the time the Shafias arrived in Canada in June 2007, the family of 10 had travelled more than halfway around the world and lived in five different countries. The older children were being educated in an English-speaking American school in Dubai. But university would be a more expensive proposition for Shafia's growing family, so they looked to Canada. Tooba had family in Montreal and they launched a two-year application process to move to Canada.

Again, Rona would be the sticking point with immigration officials. She spent several months back in Europe after the family left for Canada, staying with her sister in France and Tooba's brother in Germany, before getting a visa. Polygamous marriages are not acknowledged in Canada so they concocted the story that Rona was a relative who helped with domestic chores around the house.

In her diary, Rona describes the last 24 hours the family spent together in Dubai, on the verge of their new life in Canada. Mohammad had already arranged to ship the family's kitchen supplies, bedding, and other household goods to Montreal. This was a family used to being on the move.

"The night of our departure, I cleared out and cleaned the kitchen and no one slept," Rona writes. "Finally, after morning prayers, everyone got up at five in the morning and prepared to leave. We had some 10 pieces of luggage and departed to the airport in two taxis. My flight was at 8:30 and theirs was at 9:00." Rona flew seven-and-a-half hours to Paris; the nine Shafias travelled 16 hours to Canada with a stopover in London.

Later, in September, Mohammad and Rona reunited in Dubai. He arranged for Rona's three-month visa to Canada and they flew to Montreal on November 6, 2007.

Until she was left behind on this latest move, Mother Rona had never been away from the family; the separation from Sahar, her own daughter adopted within the family, would have been especially hard. And though the reunion in Canada was largely a happy one, Rona describes a frosty reception from Tooba, who soon informed Rona she should have stayed with her family in France and that her time in Canada probably wouldn't last long.

For years, Tooba had worked to wrest control of the family finances from Rona and supplant her in Mohammad's bed. The few months already spent in Canada, where Tooba was officially listed as Shafia's only wife, had cemented Tooba's matriarchal dominance in the household.

"She would make me so miserable and upset," Rona writes in her diary. "Sometimes she wouldn't speak to me, so I would go and speak with her because she had my passport. Tooba used to say, 'Your life is in my hands.'"

# Family life...

THE transition to life in Montreal wasn't easy for the family. The children had to attend a French-language school even though they had studied at an English-language school in Dubai. Rona spoke French but had few social opportunities to use her linguistic skills. Mohammad and Tooba spoke virtually no English and no French. The children, as happens in many immigrant families, became the official interpreters.

Before they left Dubai, the family had also made a pact: no one was to date until they finished their education. When they were old enough, they could marry. In the meantime, no dating.

Hamed seemed to have no problem with this rule. He wanted to study business in college. As the oldest son, his path seemed clear: he would likely enter the family business of importing and exporting. By the age of 18, he was hopping planes on his own and heading to Dubai to meet up with his father. His command of English meant he would conduct the online sales. He was arranging for tradespeople to do work at the $2 million family-owned shopping plaza in Laval. Plus he had a driver's licence.

His older sister Zainab did none of these things. Her freedom was severely restricted and monitored. She never learned to drive and never had a driver's licence. But neither Zainab nor her younger sister Sahar subscribed to the family's monastic existence. They liked western fashion. They enjoyed socializing. They liked being in the company of boys and flirting and falling in and out of love, like most teens their age. These desires would result in serious repercussions for them and created ugly conflict within the household.

# Sahar...

WITH their voices silenced beneath the frigid waters of the Rideau Canal, it was left to a handful of witnesses from various parts of their lives to speak for the three Shafia daughters at the murder trial of the girls' parents and brother.

Sahar Shafia was the second oldest daughter of Mohammad and Tooba Shafia, given by her mother to Rona to raise forty days after her birth. By all reports a favourite of her father, the beautiful Sahar had thick dark hair, clear skin, warm brown eyes, and perfectly shaped eyebrows. But in photographs, there is often a faraway look in her eyes, as if she were dreaming of another life.

On November 23, 2011, a vice-principal at Antoine-de Saint-Exupéry school in Montreal, Josée Fortin, took the witness stand to recount a disturbing meeting she had with Sahar.

Staff had alerted Fortin on May 7, 2008, to possible problems the girl may have been facing at home. Fortin had trained as a social worker before becoming a teacher. "What I do recall is we'd spoken initially about the wearing of the veil," Fortin recalled. "She found it very difficult to wear the veil."

Then the interview took a much more serious turn. Sahar, 16 at the time, told Fortin about a suicide attempt she had made just 10 days earlier, using pills. Sahar told the vice-principal: "I wanted to die. I had enough. I wanted to die." Sahar related other troubling details about her home life. She told Fortin that since October 2007, around the time of her 16th birthday, she had been "emotionally rejected within the family" and had little contact with other family members.

The ostracism would have begun just a month before Rona, her adoptive mother within the family, was cleared to rejoin the family in Canada. "Within the family there was an order issued that they should not talk to her," said Fortin.

Sahar also complained that her older brother, Hamed, had physically abused her on two occasions — once hitting her and another time pushing a pair of scissors across a table that struck her in the arm. Fortin testified that she did note an injury on Sahar's arm.

"She didn't feel well from an emotional standpoint," the vice-principal recalled, describing the case as rating "emergency one status." Teacher Antonella Enea had also been sitting in on the interview. Fortin decided to seek assistance from Batshaw Youth and Family Centres, the English-language service for youth protection in Montreal.

She telephoned the agency, which put intake worker Evelyn Benayoun on the line with Sahar to let the girl explain her situation. "Sahar told me she wanted to die because she was extremely sad," said Benayoun. "There wasn't just one problem. There was the suicide. There was the physical abuse."

A Batshaw social worker, Jeanne Rowe, arrived at the school that afternoon to talk to Sahar. Fortin couldn't recall who got there first, the parents or the social worker.

"Sahar had visual contact with her mother and father and brother," said Fortin. "It seems [that] she saw them and I saw a child that started changing — going back on what she said ... I noticed this change of attitude. The change of attitude surprised me and I was wondering, do I have before me a child that [is] afraid?"

She distinctly remembered Mohammad Shafia coming through the school door, looking like a storm cloud. "the parents were very angry about the complaint that was relayed to the youth protection agency," said Fortin.

Then Mohammad, as he would do with Geoff Dempster in his first interview with Kingston Police after his daughters' deaths, proclaimed he was a successful businessman and a good provider for his children.

"The father says he's worked hard for his children," recounted Fortin, "that he's building a house on the south shore."

From her first meeting alone with the girl that May 7, Batshaw child protection worker Jeanne Rowe, who had more than 20 years of experience in the field, classified Sahar's case as "code one," meaning: "It's very urgent and you have to investigate it the same day," said Rowe during her court appearance.

"When I met her she was very scared. She was crying and really didn't want to meet. She didn't give me any information," added Rowe. "She was very, very scared about her parents knowing about the report."

Sahar began recanting what she'd told her vice-principal and teacher. The rejection and alienation in the family? Not true. The suicide attempt? Not true. The physical and verbal abuse by Hamed? Again, not true.

"Everything in the report, she denied in that first meeting," said Rowe. "I went over those allegations with her and she denied them all." Throughout the half-hour interview, Sahar was described by Rowe as inconsolable and crying "profusely."

Rowe then recalled Tooba arriving at the school along with Zainab. The mother and social worker met and Rowe repeated the allegations Sahar had made to the school staff. Tooba told her that she wasn't aware of any rejection by the family, only that Sahar wanted to be left alone much of the time. She wasn't aware of her daughter's having taken pills. "She adamantly denied that Hamed was physically or verbally abusing Sahar," said Rowe.

Rowe also asked about a three-week period during which Sahar didn't attend school. Tooba explained that she and Shafia had taken their daughter on a two-week trip to Dubai. When they returned, she was too tired to go back to school so they let Sahar stay home for another week.

Rowe said she had finished talking to Tooba, then Zainab, and was leaving the school when Mohammad arrived. "He was quite angry," said Rowe. "He wanted to know the source of the report. He said he would speak to his lawyer to find out the source of the report."

Again, all of Sahar's earlier allegations were dismissed, this time by her father. "Everything he denied very openly. He didn't give me any explanations for anything," said Rowe.

Shafia flatly rejected the idea that Hamed had any authority to discipline his siblings. It was Hamed who provided the translation between his father and the social worker. Rowe asked Hamed about Sahar's allegations against him. "He denied everything," she said. But in a household as patriarchal as the Shafias', with Mohammad away for long periods of time, it's not surprising that Hamed, the eldest son, would stand in for his father in the role of disciplinarian and "protector" of his sisters.

The next day, May 8, Sahar was back at school. Rowe returned on the 9th to interview the girl. The transformation was remarkable. "She was not crying. She was seemingly happy. She was wearing the hijab. The first meeting she was not wearing the hijab," said Rowe.

Sahar also admitted for the first time to Rowe that she had, indeed, taken pills. She said she sometimes became sad. "She said, I didn't want to kill myself. I was just sad.'" She claimed that she merely slept off the effects of the pills.

"She was happier – or seemingly happier," recalled Rowe, though she felt Sahar was being "very cautious and minimized the situation." Sahar had also spoken to her mother, who told her daughter she must always come and talk to her when she was feeling sad. "And she told her brother the hitting must stop."

# Zainab...

BEFORE these eruptions at school in the spring of 2008, there had been another incident at the home on rue Bonnivet that threw the family into turmoil and pitted siblings against one another.

Zainab Shafia, Mohammad and Tooba's first child, was a gorgeous young woman. All the Shafia children were striking, with their dark hair, clear complexions, and penetrating eyes, but beautiful Zainab had a sultry look in her almond-shaped brown eyes, and her lips were full and heart-shaped. She liked to dress fashionably and take pictures of herself — some of them sexy and provocative — on her cellphone. At her English-language high school, Zainab had caught the attention of Ammar Wahid, a young man of Pakistani heritage. Like many smitten young men before him, Ammar went way out on a limb on February 14, 2008.

"It was Valentine's Day so I sent her a Valentine's card," he recalled in court two and a half years later. "I wrote a little note saying I kinda liked her."

Ammar got what he wanted — a response from Zainab. But it wasn't what he expected. Instead of an OK for a date or some kind of meeting, he received an e-mail from her, outlining the "rules of friendship." Above all else, they had to avoid the prying eyes of Zainab's younger brother, Hamed, who also went to their school.

She e-mailed Ammar: "Be aware of my bro... and if my bro is

around act like a complete stranger. I will call u when we r at skool from the public telephone."

Meeting up was difficult because of the restrictions on Zainab's freedom, even though she was 18 at the time. "During the weekend it was kind of tough to see her because she was not allowed to go out," said Ammar.

Ammar received other e-mails from Zainab, giving him careful instructions. If Hamed was at her locker, Ammar was not to come around. "I don't want to give him the slightest idea we are friends," she wrote.

About a month after the start of their clandestine relationship, Zainab invited Ammar to her house. Her parents were in Dubai with Sahar. Rona was in the home; Zainab introduced her to Ammar as her "dad's sister." Then, Zainab suddenly realized that Hamed was coming home.

"As soon as I walked in the house she told me to hide in the basement," Ammar told the court. "I was hiding behind a box and her brother directly came and saw me there." It was a strange encounter. Hamed walked up to his sister's boyfriend, shook his hand, then asked him to leave.

Ammar walked away and called a friend to come pick him up. He contacted Zainab on his cellphone. "She just said, 'Leave, don't come back now. He's pissed and he wants to come after you.'"

Zainab never returned to school. "Her brother told her until her father and mother came back, he wasn't allowing her to go," said Ammar. "She told me her brother's not letting her out [to] do anything. He's just keeping her at home."

Hamed continued to go to school and the two young men would pass in the hallway.

"We wouldn't talk or anything," said Ammar. "We just looked at each other and walked away. That was pretty much that."

With their relationship interrupted, Zainab and Ammar corresponded occasionally by e-mail. She said she wanted to see him again. He wanted to see her, too. She was going to night school, but not alone. She was accompanied by Hamed and she was wearing the hijab. But in an e-mail to Ammar dated December 5, 2008, Zainab showed some of the independent spirit that probably got her killed. She wrote: "I wear at nite coz i go to a coarse at nigh with him sux/ well i changed the way i wear hijab its even more better than be4/ i take out a bit of ma hair and i tie the hijab at back and put on some big circle earings."

In the spring of 2009, Zainab and Ammar arranged a meeting at the library. Sahar was there and they all went for lunch at a McDonald's. "She told me her dad was mad at her for what she did. That's why they took her out of school," Ammar recalled her saying. "It took some time for them to forgive her so she could go back to school." Zainab said she was spending most of her time in her room, only coming out for meals.

Their friendship rekindled, Ammar and Zainab began making plans. "You help me and we'll leave together," she told him. Ammar said he needed a job first, then he would get an apartment for them.

But Zainab was in a hurry.

# Zainab's escape...

APRIL 17, 2009, was a day of utter turmoil in the Shafia household. Tooba had come home to find a note from Zainab, saying she was leaving home and didn't want any contact with them. Ammar had come earlier in the day to take her to a women's shelter, Passages, a refuge for women aged 18 to 30 having difficulties in their lives with issues such as violence or drug abuse. Zainab was interviewed by Passages worker Jennifer Bumbray that afternoon and officially classified as a victim of "family violence."

"I do remember her speaking of physical violence by her brother," Bumbray recalled at the trial. Zainab also talked about conflicts with her father. "She didn't feel safe. She was being sequestered in her house and wasn't allowed to go to school."

The social workers at Passages didn't know what to make of this lovely, open young woman with apparently ample spending money and nice clothes. "She wasn't our typical clientele. She seemed to be well off. She came in with expensive clothing. She was very friendly," said Bumbray.

Zainab was admitted to Passages, underwent the standard search of her luggage, and was read the house rules. The instructions on her admittance sheet stipulated no communication with family members. Ammar was listed as her emergency contact. For Zainab, the experience was liberating. She could come and go as she wished. Ammar acted as the go-between with her family.

The scene at rue Bonnivet, meanwhile, was deteriorating. Four of the Shafia children had learned of Zainab's sudden departure on April 17 through a phone call from their mother. Feeling anxious and upset, they walked up to a stranger on the street and said they were afraid to go home and that their lives were in danger. Police were called and officers arrived to speak to the children before driving them home around 4 pm. Tooba and Hamed were at the house. Police were concerned about the report they'd gotten from the four children but Hamed and Tooba were preoccupied with Zainab's disappearance.

Earlier in the day, at 3:52 pm, Hamed had placed a call to the 911 Montreal police emergency line to report Zainab missing. In the call, Hamed tells the 911 operator that his sister was 19 years old, had been gone since the morning, and had left a note saying she was going away and not returning.

The operator asks Hamed if his sister has been having problems. His answers are vague, and police are dispatched to the house to talk to him.

At 4:06 pm, Hamed called the 911 line again: "Hello, uh, I just asked for the police car, uh, police cars and, uh, they didn't come yet," he says.

Again he explained that his older sister, who wasn't suicidal and didn't take drugs, simply walked away from the house that morning and left a note saying so. In a city of more than two million, this incident had to be low on the police list of priorities.

Later that evening, while everyone was in the living room with the police, the children revealed they were suffering abuse and violence in the home. Sahar, Geeti, and two of their other siblings were brought outside by police, one at a time, to talk.

Constable Anne-Marie Choquette, one of the investigating officers, supplied an agreed statement of fact for the trial. "Geeti disclosed an incident that had happened the week before, when she and her siblings had been at a shopping centre and were coming home late," Choquette wrote. "She told police that her father had pulled her hair and hit her on the face. She told police that her brother Hamed hit her in the eye with his fist. Geeti also told police that her father often threatened that he was going to kill them. No marks were observed on Geeti."

The revelations began pouring from Sahar and Geeti: slapping by Hamed and violence against Zainab by their father. Sahar and Geeti said they wanted to be taken out of the home because they feared their father.

Then Mohammad Shafia arrived home. "The demeanour of the children changed when Shafia arrived home," wrote Choquette. "After his arrival, the children stopped talking. Some of the children were crying." He spoke to the children in Farsi, which the officers could not understand.

At around 9 that night, a child protection worker arrived at the home. The discussion continued for some time, mostly in English, occasionally in French, with the children translating for the parents.

At around 11 pm, Child and Family Services chose not to take action. Despite all they had seen and heard, the social worker decided that the children would stay in the home for the weekend and the interviews would resume on Monday. In Quebec, criminal charges in such situations are determined by Child and Family Services workers. No charges were ever laid. Two and a half months later, Montreal police would be assisting in a mass murder investigation.

Questions would be asked after the trial about whether Montreal child protection services could have acted differently, perhaps by intervening and removing some of the children from the home. In what was clearly a sensitive situation involving a clash of cultures, were case workers being too respectful of authoritarian traditions and behaviours? Was it a mistake to ask the children to explain their situation in the presence of their parents, especially when they had stated they were afraid of their father?

The Shafia case, in which a conflict between teenagers and parents emphasized competing cultural values — with the daughters choosing to behave in a more modern Canadian way than their parents could tolerate — has fuelled concerns about the reluctance to adapt by some more conservative immigrants, and the need to move forward and take action even if the family isn't willing to accept intervention.

Zainab would stay at passages for two weeks. Meanwhile, Hamed and Mohammad were beside themselves. They desperately wanted to find Zainab and bring her home.

On April 19, two days after the interview at rue Bonnivet, Constable Choquette arrived at the police station to find the two men waiting for her. Did she have any information about Zainab's whereabouts? Hamed said he had managed to get Ammar's cellphone number but that Ammar wasn't answering.

"They wanted something to be done. They absolutely wanted to find Zainab," Choquette testified. She said she would try Ammar's number.

When Choquette talked to Ammar, he assured her Zainab was fine and that her departure was entirely voluntary. She was of age, after all.

71

The phone calls continued. Ammar stalled. Mohammad and Hamed grew more impatient. "At one point," Ammar said, "the father said, if you don't tell us where she is, we're going to go to the police to make a complaint against you." That's when Zainab and Ammar made a trip to the police station for her to report in person that she was safe and had left her home because she didn't want to be there. Police told the Shafia men to back off.

# The wedding...

THE parents' and Hamed's strategy then shifted. They decided to let Tooba negotiate with Zainab. A meeting was arranged between mother and daughter at a neutral location, the old courthouse in Montreal. Ammar also went. This 19th century monument to justice, on rue Notre-Dame in Old Montreal, seems like an odd place to set the meeting. However, it is a very public area, near souvenir shops, a tourist information office, and two public squares, Place Vauquelin and Place Jacques-Cartier. Perhaps Zainab hoped her mother would contain her emotions, surrounded by tourists and strangers, or perhaps she feared being dragged off by her angry father and brother, and chose to take no chances.

Tooba pleaded with Zainab to come home. Zainab refused, knowing how angry her father would be. Tooba told Zainab and Ammar that she would get an apartment so she and her daughters could move out of the house. Despite Zainab's suspicions, Ammar thought Tooba was sincere. "A mother's always a mother," he believed.

Then Tooba upped the ante. If Zainab came home, she would help arrange her marriage to Ammar. Zainab stayed at the shelter for another week. On May 2, she went home. Not coincidentally, her father had left the day before on another one of his extended business trips to Dubai. He would be gone for several weeks.

May 18 was set as the date for Ammar and Zainab's wedding,

though no one in the family liked the idea of her marrying outside the Afghan community, especially to a young man who had no job, no money, no apparent family support, and what they suspected was a problem with drugs and alcohol. They had also heard a rumour that Ammar was engaged to a young woman in Pakistan, arranged by his family. Ammar has always denied this.

In order to have a religious wedding in the Muslim tradition, Tooba and Hamed would have to find a mullah to conduct the ceremony. Because they did not attend a mosque, they had to enlist the help of Tooba's uncle, Latif Hyderi, who lived not too far from the Shafias. This was a delicate business within the family system, however. Not long after the Shafias came to Montreal in June of 2007, Latif had suggested an arranged marriage between Zainab and his own son, Hussain. Zainab and Hussain were second cousins. The arrangement was rebuffed. Tooba told her uncle that Zainab was too young to marry and needed to finish her education.

Though the two families had limited contact after that incident, the Shafias were now desperate. Uncle Latif agreed to help. He even went to the mosque on May 18 with Tooba and Hamed to see Zainab and Ammar being married. Latif's other son, Reza, was there as a witness.

Following tradition, the celebration was to take place the next day at an Iranian restaurant booked by Tooba and Hamed. The family took Zainab back home that evening where the scene was anything but joyous.

"Everybody, their hearts were bleeding," said Latif. There were concerns about Zainab marrying "a foreigner." Latif tried to lighten the mood by putting on some music and exhorting everyone to dance. "I told her I'm happy and congratulated her."

More trouble was brewing, however. Ammar had warned Zainab that his family was also unhappy about the marriage. Tooba and Hamed asked Ammar who from his family would be at the celebration. No one, he said. The Shafias, once again, went into crisis mode. Family honour would be at stake when relatives started to ask questions about the groom's family. Tooba told her uncle that Hamed was so upset she feared he would hit someone.

"Hamed tried to find someone," Ammar recalled. "He asked me to find someone that could act like my family." Hamed even suggested someone could play the role of Ammar's parents for the day. Remarkably, no one seemed concerned about the most glaring absence of all — the bride's father, Mohammad Shafia, who was paying for the wedding but was out of the country and totally out of the picture.

The celebration was anything but celebratory. It was, in fact, a total disaster. Ammar arrived with another young man of indeterminate status, which didn't appease anyone. Extended Shafia family members began whispering, scandalized by the non-appearance of Ammar's family. Tooba was beside herself with embarrassment. "Tooba was under pressure. She was crying," said Latif.

Zainab started crying, too, and that was too much for Tooba, who fainted. Zainab told Latif the only reason she was marrying Ammar was to get out of the house, away from the abuse, with a plan to then take her sisters away, too. She said: "Uncle, this boy doesn't have money and he's not handsome. The only reason I'm marrying him is to get my revenge. I will sacrifice myself for my sisters. At least they will get their freedom after me." But the scene with Tooba in the restaurant broke her resolve.

"Zainab, she threw herself on the chest of her mom and

was crying," Latif recalled. "She said, 'I reject this one. I will reject this boy.'"

By now, the mullah who had married the couple was also asking why there was so much confusion. They explained that Zainab wanted to annul the marriage. He agreed to undo it, but by then Ammar was nowhere to be found. Zainab had already told him she couldn't go through with the marriage.

"She was crying," Ammar recalled. "I just told her I completely respect [it] if that's what you want. We'll break off the marriage. I just left."

This created more confusion. If the marriage was to be annulled, the groom had to be brought back to the restaurant. Hamed jumped in the family car and went searching for him. Hamed wasn't about to let this opportunity pass — a chance to get rid of Ammar, the Pakistani interloper, once and for all.

Hamed found Ammar at a subway station and dragged him back to the restaurant where the mullah presided over the annulment of the brief marriage. To make it official, Ammar and Zainab merely had to repeat the word "divorce" three times. They did and it was all over.

Food was served but no one had an appetite. Family gathered at the Shafia home to console Tooba. Eventually, the food went to the Hyderis and everyone went there to eat. During the bitter feast, Hussain Hyderi arrived home, oblivious to the mayhem that had just occurred. According to Latif, Tooba said to Hussain that it was he who should have started a relationship with Zainab. Hussain told his cousin he would consider it, but only if Zainab were agreeable. "I have to talk to the girl personally. If we agree, both of us, I will marry her," Latif recalled his son saying.

A couple of days later, Latif and Hussain went to the Shafias. "He's a shy boy. He's not a boy who went out with the girls," said Latif.

Hamed was clearly the Shafia power broker in his father's absence, announcing that he was prepared to start the engagement process. The family went outside so Zainab and Hussain could talk. After about 20 minutes, the young couple announced that the engagement could move ahead. No one really knows what was going on in Zainab's mind at this point. Did she really want to marry her cousin Hussain, or was this just another way for her to get out of her father's house with a more acceptable husband?

There was only one thing left to do: the fathers, Mohammad and Latif, would talk. Latif got Mohammad's phone number from Hamed so he could make the call to Dubai. The response wasn't what Latif had expected.

# Sahar and Geeti...

IN February 2009, troubles flared up once more at Antoine-de Saint-Exupéry school for Geeti and Sahar. This time, Vice-principal Nathalie Laramée was in charge of their files. Laramée had taught a class for immigrant children coming to Canada who needed to study in French. She knew four of the seven Shafia children — Sahar, Geeti, and two other siblings who cannot be identified because of an ongoing court ban.

The school had been trying to set up a meeting with Tooba and Mohammad to discuss the girls' behaviour, particularly their chronic lateness and absenteeism. When she met with Laramée, Tooba said she was at a loss as to what to do with the girls.

"The mother asked me to help her out," said Laramée. The vice-principal warned Tooba that child protection workers would be called again if there was no change. Attendance improved for a couple of months.

By April, the situation had deteriorated once more with Zainab's disappearance. A family conference took place at the school involving Mohammad, Tooba, Sahar, Geeti, and the younger brother. As well as the girls' usual absenteeism, the brother wasn't completing his homework. Laramée recalled Mohammad Shafia's anger.

"The father was speaking very loudly in my office and saying, 'What can we do? What can we do?'" said Laramée. The children were interpreting for their father but she noticed he kept saying something about "police." When the parents left, the brother explained that the police had been at their house on April 17 — but that things at home were improving.

When the brother left the office, Laramée recalled the conversation taking "a different bent" once more. Sahar and Geeti accused their brother of not telling the truth about how things were at home. Sahar told the vice-principal she didn't translate everything her father was saying because of his lies. "My sister and I are afraid in the house," Laramée recalled Sahar saying to her.

The vice-principal also told court about another perplexing incident that April. Sahar was supposed to go on a school trip to a sugar bush. She showed up late and refused to go along. Sahar told Laramée that Zainab had been in a car accident.

"Sahar explained to me that she was very preoccupied that her sister Zainab had been hospitalized and she was very worried about her," Laramée said. "She wished also to go see her. She did not want to take part in the sugar bush activity."

Of course Sahar would be worried about Zainab and want to see her. But it was a lie. Her older sister wasn't in hospital, but had been hiding out at the women's shelter, leaving the family in total flux.

On May 11, Geeti was expelled from school. She had had a run-in with her teacher and Laramée went to talk with her. "It was a hard lunch hour because Geeti was crying," Laramée said. "Geeti was very angry with her teacher." The teacher had spoken with Sahar who revealed a plot the girls had hatched to leave their home and go live on their own. When the teacher explained that it wasn't possible, that Geeti was too young, Geeti exploded.

Thirteen-year-old Geeti, Mohammad and Tooba's sixth child (two other children, who cannot be named, were born between Sahar and Geeti), was the most defiant of the Shafia sisters. Closely resembling her mother Tooba in looks, Geeti also seemed to have inherited Tooba's strong will. She had told police she wanted to be out of the house and she wanted to be able to go out freely like her friends. She even asked to be placed with a foster family.

The 75-minute interview with Geeti was difficult for Laramée. "I was also crying because I didn't know what to do anymore," she said. "Many events were piling up on each other."

Over the course of the 2008-09 academic year, Geeti had missed 40 classes and was late 30 times. She had to be sent home one day for wearing a revealing sweater, makeup, and earrings considered inappropriate for a 13-year-old. "She was failing in all of her courses," said Laramée. "Things were going downhill fast. Geeti was practically not going to school."

Geeti only wanted her freedom and to be with her beautiful older sister Sahar. The youngest of the four victims, Geeti was very close to Sahar. At the trial, the Crown presented a page of messages Geeti had written to Sahar, tragically poignant in hindsight: "i wish 2 god dat till im alive i'll never see u sad," she wrote. "i dont know if one day you leave this house wat am i gonna do????" "i promise before dying i'll make all ur wishes cum true one by one." As for the message in the centre of page, Geeti ultimately got her wish: "i hope we'll never be separted [sic]."

There were even darker family dynamics at play, inside and outside the home. Sahar told Laramée that her younger brother was spying on her at school. He didn't like her friends and threatened to tell their father "she was a whore." Sahar would leave the house in the morning wearing long sweaters and modest clothes. At school she would put on makeup and earrings and more revealing clothes. She changed again before going home in the afternoon.

Antonella Enea was one of Sahar's teachers during the 2007-08 school year at Antoine- de Saint-Exupéry. She was with Sahar and the vice-principal when the girl made her disclosures of abuse and the suicide attempt. It was at Enea's prompting that she did so. Enea had become Sahar's confidante and was extremely concerned for the girl.

"At one point in time she told me no one spoke to her at her place," said Enea. "She said she couldn't have a normal life of a young girl, see her friends, things of that nature." Sahar also told Enea that nothing could be done to help her as she talked about the ostracism and physical abuse she was experiencing.

"It was during that time that she also told me she had taken medication — lots of medication," said Enea. One of the sisters was at home and went to their mother to tell Tooba about the trouble Sahar was in. Tooba told the sister not to bother her about Sahar. It was her "aunt" who came to her assistance — Rona, her adopted mother. According to Rona's diary, Tooba said, "She can go to hell. Let her kill herself." The story was enough for Enea, who took Sahar to Vice-principal Fortin to make the report to social workers.

In 2008-09, Enea had less contact with Sahar, though she did occasionally teach her. In June of 2009, she found Sahar to be desperately afraid. "She told me that her father was supposed to come back from a trip and she was afraid her brother ... was going to tell her father she was a whore," said Enea. "I said, 'Do you want me to do something?' She said, 'Yes.'"

Enea called child protection authorities once more. The

agency told her to take Sahar to the school psychologist and arrange to find her a shelter. Enea said they found some shelters but, for some reason, Sahar never went to one. The school year was winding down fast and, when Sahar met with a school psychologist, the talk turned to how to get a job, not about finding a safe place of refuge.

# Sahar's boyfriend...

W HY would Sahar's younger brother accuse her of being a whore? By June of 2009, Sahar had a steady boyfriend named Ricardo Sanchez whom she had been dating for about four months. Sahar saw Ricardo as her ticket out of the oppressive household. There had already been suspicion about whether Sahar was dating. Sometime during the 2007-08 school year, Tooba went to the school to talk to teacher Claudia Deslauriers. One of Sahar's younger sisters was there to translate for their mother.

"The mother came to see us to determine if Sahar had kissed a boy — whether she had a boyfriend," Deslauriers recalled. "She seemed to be really angry."

Deslauriers had seen Sahar at school with a boy but she was concerned about giving Tooba this information. The teacher and Sahar had already spoken on one occasion about bruises and scratches she had seen on the girl's arms and told her no one had a right to harm her. Deslauriers weighed how forthcoming she should be with Tooba.

"I told her that no, she didn't kiss any boy. I didn't want Sahar to encounter any problems after our meeting," Deslauriers said. "The mother said to us that she did not accept that her daughter would have kissed a boy, as it was not falling within the parameters of her values."

By June 2009, Sahar was in a full-blown relationship with Ricardo, a native of Honduras and about three years her senior. Zainab knew Ricardo from night school, where they were learning French, and had introduced him to her sister.

Ricardo's nickname for Sahar was "Natasha." That's what she told him her name was when they first met and it was some time before she revealed her true name.

One time he, too, noticed bruises on Sahar's leg and arm. She said she had fallen at school but Ricardo wasn't buying her story. He thought the marks looked like they had been produced by a blow — "like when somebody hits you." Sahar never told Ricardo the same stories of abuse she had told her teachers. All he knew was that their relationship had to be a secret, owing, he thought, to their religious differences.

Their time together was also limited by the curfews Sahar's parents had placed on their children. She was frustrated and hatched a plan with Ricardo to run away to Honduras and live with his family — even though he realized his Catholic parents would be as upset about his marrying a Muslim as Sahar's would be about her seeing a Catholic.

One person who learned of the depth of Sahar's concern about her parents was Ricardo's aunt, Erma Medina. For quite a while, Medina also believed Sahar's name was Natasha, until the girl told her otherwise. She wanted to know more about this beautiful young woman her nephew was dating, and one day she asked Sahar about her home life.

Sahar told Medina that "the day her parents knew about her relationship with Ricardo she would be a dead woman. She told me several times. All the time she was talking to me, she was serious."

In April 2009, at a birthday gathering with Ricardo's family, Sahar had revealed she was going to tell her parents about her boyfriend and their plan to move to Honduras. Medina was asked in court why Sahar would do so, knowing it would cause serious trouble for her. "Because she loved Ricardo," the aunt replied. "She told me she would love him until death."

There was a particularly close call one day as the couple was sitting in a restaurant with a girlfriend of Sahar's. In walked Sahar's younger brother, whose identity cannot be revealed due to a court publication ban.

"I was embracing Sahar," Ricardo recalled. "When she saw he was coming she said to stop embracing her because this boy didn't know about our relationship. He arrived and he started to ask if Sahar was my girlfriend. Later I told him she wasn't my girlfriend — that we just met."

Sahar looked scared. Her girlfriend told the brother that Ricardo was her boyfriend, not Sahar's. But that wasn't good enough. The boy was suspicious — and persistent.

"He told me I had to prove it," said Ricardo, who described him as "really pressing, like a kid that needs candy."

"I had to grab the other girl and kiss her in front of him."

There was some normalcy when the two couples — Sahar and Ricardo, Zainab and Ammar — double-dated, occasionally going out to a movie or to a restaurant. One time, Sahar even introduced Ricardo to Geeti at school as her boyfriend. "She was normal. She didn't say anything," said Ricardo of the little sister.

In court on November 29, 2011, Ricardo Sanchez was asked to read a sampling of the love texts he had sent to Sahar in the days and weeks before her death. They were recovered from Sahar's phone that was found in the Nissan Sentra after it was lifted from the bottom of the Rideau Canal.

Ricardo sent one of the texts to her just two days before she set out on the family trip. "The only thing I would wish in this world is to have you every day of my life. The world is very large and one day I could even lose you," the young man read in Spanish. "But in this world as large as it is there's a small heart and you can never get lost in that one heart because it's only for you, my love."

Ricardo was unable to read the entire message in the hushed courtroom without crying and stopping to control his emotions. Not a sound could be heard but the young man's quiet voice.

In the darkness of the back seat of the Nissan the night of June 29, as they drove toward home along Highway 401, Sahar texted Ricardo to say she was with Rona, Zainab, and Geeti. They were just two or three hours away from Montreal but the decision had been made to stop at Kingston for the night.

"Their father had told them they were gonna stop at a hotel because they were tired," Ricardo testified. "All she said was that she found it very strange they were in that car and their father was in a different car."

# Zainab's

# engagement...

LATIF Hyderi made his courtesy phone call to Mohammad Shafia in Dubai in May 2009 — the father of the prospective groom
paying his respects to the father of the bride and seeking permission
to go ahead with the marriage arrangement. Everything seemed
to be going well on the Montreal end. Tooba and Hamed were on
board. The young people themselves seemed content. Hussain had a
good management job at a Montreal grocery store. He could provide
for Zainab. But what Latif heard over the phone from Dubai unnerved him.

"I [had] asked her hand for Hussain and they agreed. We
are waiting for your [Mohammad's] opinion," Latif recalled telling
Shafia. "He said, 'Just wait until I come.' He was angry."

Shafia, though indicating he was agreeable to the marriage,
demanded that there be no contact between Zainab and Hussain for
now.

Latif was stung. "Your honour is my honour," he pointed out
to Shafia. His son was willing to marry Zainab who had shamed the
family with her broken marriage to Ammar. Latif and his family, in
other words, were doing Shafia a favour.

Shafia was preoccupied with Zainab's behaviour. Latif couldn't believe what he heard next. "He said, If I was there, I would have killed her.'"

Latif was perplexed. "Why do you want to do that? She is a child," he told Shafia. "Children make mistakes. Don't show yourself [to be] that angry. Your problem is solved." One way of restoring honour1 to the family is by marrying the "offending" woman off. The marriage is supposed to be with the person who violated her honour — even if she has been raped by him — but marrying the woman to someone else is an acceptable alternative.

According to Latif, Shafia could not be appeased. When Latif persisted in seeking permission for the marriage arrangement, Shafia accused the older man of trying to get at his wealth through marriage.

"I said, I have no eyes for your money. It's just for the humanity of this girl and the honour of this girl,'" Latif replied.

According to Latif's account, Shafia abruptly hung up the phone. They never talked again about the matter.

"I was worried why Shafia ... he's talking this way," Latif said.

Latif decided to go to Tooba's brother, Ahmed Javid, who lived in the same area of Montreal. Ahmed arranged for Tooba to come to his house for a meeting with Latif. Latif insisted that she come alone. He felt biased information was getting to Shafia. "Shafia used to get the message very fast," he said. "That's why I wanted to talk to Tooba alone. I had suspicion of Hamed."

When Hamed appeared for the meeting with his mother, Latif decided to tackle the problem head-on. He sat Hamed down on

1    http://www.meforum.org/50/honor-murders-why-the-perps-get-off-easy

88

the verandah for a talk. You're really a good boy, he told Hamed, but your family is fixed on too many old traditions. He also knew that Hamed had too much control over the girls, including Zainab, who was older than her brother. "You have five sisters," Latif said. "You should make yourself friends to your sisters. You should work with your sister[s] like a close friend."

Latif decided to send a message to Shafia through the son: Lighten up. Let the sisters go to parties. Let them associate freely with friends.

"Maybe your father doesn't understand the environment," Latif told him. "Your sisters can't watch TV. They're like political prisoners. This is completely against humanity, against the situation in this country."

Latif said Hamed listened quietly as they sat on the front porch. In a few days, the young man would pack his black suitcase and fly off to join his father in Dubai for 12 days.

# Rona's life...

WHILE the Shafia girls were feeling the heavy hand of parental control in June of 2009, pressure was building on Rona. Isolation was increasing inside the household and she had no network of friends in Montreal.

When Rona first came to Canada in November 2007, the Hyderis invited her to their house, along with Tooba and Shafia, for the traditional meal given to travellers. Latif told her to consider him her "paternal uncle."

"You can always come to our house. Don't feel isolated that you have no brother or sister here or no parents here," he recalled telling her. "She became very happy when I told her these things."

The Hyderis didn't have much contact with Rona after that, except to see her when she walked past their home on her many endless, solitary walks, in all seasons and all weather.

One day, on leaving their apartment building, they were surprised to find Tooba outside with one of the children. "Don't talk to Rona," Latif recalled her saying. "Don't talk to Rona at all." The Hyderis could only come to one conclusion about this unsettling demand — things were happening in the Shafia household that someone didn't want known.

The Hyderis would walk in a neighbourhood park also frequented by Rona. It would later be revealed that she used a pay telephone there to make secret calls to supportive friends and family members. The Hyderis would say hello but felt uncomfortable since Tooba had confronted them. "There are always problems in their house," Latif told his wife. "We should give up coming to this park."

One day, however, Latif was alone in the park and met Rona. "She said, I wanted to talk to you. I have a problem I want to talk to you about if you will listen to me. There is a lot of cruelty and oppression practised on me by Tooba and Shafia. They beat me two or three times. I am as their servant, not a wife,'" Latif testified in court.

Tooba and Shafia had her immigration documents. She was constantly uncertain of her legal status in Canada. Rona didn't realize it, but the Montreal immigration lawyer Shafia had hired to handle her case also had concerns.

Sabine Venturelli, like everyone else outside the family, believed Rona Amir Mohammad to be Shafia's cousin. Twice, she had arranged to have Rona's visitor's visa extended. The last one was due to expire on August 30, 2009, and this time, if she was instructed by Shafia to proceed, Venturelli would file for Rona's permanent immigrant status based on humanitarian grounds.

What Venturelli recalled in court was that Rona never appeared at her office without one or both Shafias and a female relative being there as well. Shafia always paid for the work with cash. By spring of 2009, Venturelli hadn't been contacted by anyone about Rona's case since the previous November.

What the jury never heard was that Shafia, through his female relative, had sent an offer to Venturelli to close the file — for a fee of $10,000. The closure likely would have resulted in Rona's being sent out of Canada. The lawyer never accepted this exorbitant sum and never performed the work. At the time of Rona's death, the file was still active at Venturelli's office and with Canadian immigration.

Rona's isolation was also increasing. According to her confidantes, the children were ordered not to talk to her. Rona said she confronted Shafia about his treatment of her. Rona was also calling her brother and sister in Europe, from the park, to ask for their advice. Her sister, Diba Masoomi, told her to divorce Shafia and come live with her in France.

Latif Hyderi was at a loss as to how to advise Rona. "I saw that I couldn't help her," he recalled. "I told Rona, My sister, do something.'"

Rona was trying to do something. By talking to Latif, she may, in fact, have been acting on the advice of a woman in the United States who had become a close long-distance telephone confidante.

Fahima Vorgetts never met Rona face to face but she did talk to her at least a hundred times in the year prior to Rona's death. Vorgetts's uncle was married to one of Rona's sisters. They became close through their telephone contacts — most of which occurred when Rona called from the phone booth in the park. She told Vorgetts that her phone time had been restricted in the home and that she was being ostracized. "Most of the time she would be crying a lot," said Vorgetts.

Rona told her long-distance friend the story of how she had married Shafia at a young age and that her inability to have children had created a chasm between her and Shafia. "She was controlled from day one, then abused," Vorgetts recounted. Vorgetts believed Rona was in very real danger posed by Shafia and his temper.

"She was afraid to stay. She was afraid to leave. He said he would find her and kill her. He did tell her many times that he will kill her. When he was abusing her, beating her up, he used that word," she said.

Vorgetts is director of the Afghan Women's Fund, which supports organizations that educate women and children and assist with health issues, particularly concerning maternal and paediatric care. She became a feminist at the age of 10 after the fundamentalist Taliban took over Afghanistan and began imposing restrictions on women. Rona had talked to Vorgetts about getting out of the Shafia home and possibly moving to the U.S., or to Europe where she had family. She said she was seeking a divorce settlement from Shafia.

"She was thinking about going to Europe, not to Afghanistan. As a divorcée, she would have a difficult time there," Vorgetts said. "A woman cannot live alone in Afghanistan. It's not uncommon, but it's looked down upon."

The last time Vorgetts spoke to Rona was at the end of April 2009. "She was controlled. At the end of our conversations, she was convinced she should leave — that she should stand on her own feet," said Vorgetts.

This was also the tumultuous period during which Zainab was in the women's shelter and the Shafia men were searching frantically to find her — before Tooba ultimately negotiated Zainab's return home.

Vorgetts believes the girls were not just being rebellious teens but sending out cries for help. Otherwise, Vorgetts asked, why did Geeti shoplift if she had everything she needed, including lots of spending money? Why would a 13-year-old wear revealing clothes to school and get kicked out as a result? Why did Zainab make the decision to go to a women's shelter? "A happy girl would not want to be in a shelter. Shelters are very foreign to Afghanistan," said Vorgetts.

Rona was witnessing firsthand with Zainab how breaking

away from the family could upset the men in the household. Still, Vorgetts was trying to get her to report the abuse to police and to seek help at a Montreal church or mosque. "She said if she goes to the police her husband will kill her," said Vorgetts. "She took it seriously. Her husband told her he will kill her if she leaves."

There were other reasons why Rona couldn't leave. "She loved the girls; she loved the children," Vorgetts said. "Another reason was, if she goes to the police, her husband threatened they would send her back to Afghanistan."

Rona said Shafia knew people in Afghanistan who would find her and kill her. Vorgetts left for Afghanistan on May 1, 2009, returning to her home in Virginia on July 1, the day after Rona's body was found in the canal. Rona had called a number of times in that month-long interval. "There were desperate messages. It sounded like she was in big trouble," Vorgetts recalled.

But Vorgetts had no way of contacting Rona. The year of calls from Montreal, sometimes coming two and three times a week, were all made by Rona from the pay phone in the park, using calling cards she bought with her allowance.

Vorgetts tried to reach her through various relatives but never did.

"I think the message did not get through to her," Vorgetts testified at the trial. "Then I heard she was dead."

# Fazil's testimony...

IT had been many years since Fazil Javid had seen his sister, Tooba. Now here they were, sitting face to face, 10 m apart, in the main courtroom of the Frontenac County Court House in Kingston. Javid had been flown in by the Crown to testify at his sister's murder trial. His testimony would play a significant role in the Shafia convictions.

Sometime around the start of 2009, Tooba had started calling her brother in Sweden where he owned a pizzeria. She needed to speak to her brother on a regular basis "about the family problems in the home ... She wanted to open up to me and talk about it," he told the court.

Tooba's main concern, according to Fazil, was Zainab's desire to marry Ammar Wahid and the tension it was creating in the home. Fazil talked to his niece twice on the phone. In fact, he tried to convince Zainab to follow her parents' advice and not marry the young Pakistani man.

They had a third encounter using Skype in April or May of 2009. "That was accidental," said Fazil. Zainab happened to be visiting Fazil's brother Ahmed at his home not far from the Shafias in Montreal. They talked to each other "maybe 10 minutes," recalled Fazil, coming close to tears on the witness stand. Sahar was also in the room with Zainab but wouldn't show herself on the computer's Web camera because she was too shy. Zainab explained to her uncle that she only wanted to marry Ammar to get away from her father.

"She was not happy and she wanted to leave the house. That's what she told me," said Fazil. "The condition was so hard on her she wanted as soon as possible to leave the house." At age 19, Zainab described not being able to wear the clothes she wanted, being forced to wear the hijab, not allowed to go out with friends or even go to the library.

"There was no permission for that. She wanted that freedom. She was fed up. She just wanted to marry," said Fazil. "There was one person and that was Mr. Shafia who was making the decisions."

Zainab also told Fazil about Hamed's role, assigned by their father, to spy on her. "He's always following me," Zainab complained.

"Zainab hated her father," Fazil said. "Shafia hated Zainab." Fazil had already told Tooba that he was unable to change Zainab's mind about marrying Ammar. He suggested now he might come to Canada and help the family sort out their problems.

As it turned out, Fazil was also getting information about the Shafias' household turmoil from another inside source — Rona. Twice she called him from the Montreal pay phone to talk about how "everything was disintegrated." He recalled Rona talking about Geeti, how the little girl was lonely and staying in Rona's room with her away from the rest of the family.

Rona was isolated. "She didn't have any authority at home like a housewife," said Fazil. According to Fazil, Rona had approached Shafia about getting a divorce and asked for a settlement of $50,000. Shafia told her he would send her to France and give her just $2,000, nothing more.

Fazil decided to float his idea of visiting Montreal with Shafia who was, as usual, working in Dubai. This was a dicey proposition.

The two had not spoken since 1992 when they were fleeing to Pakistan and the two men had a disagreement over the ownership of one of the vehicles they were driving. Shafia considered him a mortal enemy because of the incident. Fazil persisted. Around the end of May or early June 2009, he got Shafia's phone number in Dubai. He placed the call from his pizza shop around 4 in the afternoon Swedish time, using a calling card because the card rates were cheaper than using the regular phone system.

Shafia seemed to be prepared for his brother-in-law's call. "He told me, I just want some help from you,'" Fazil told the court.

According to Fazil, Shafia tried to engage his help "to fulfill the murder plan of Zainab." Shocked, Fazil listened as Shafia, sounding extremely angry, revealed his plot to have Tooba, Zainab, and one of the younger sisters travel to Sweden for a visit. While they were there, Shafia would show up and one day they would all travel to the seaside for a family barbecue. Shafia would lure Zainab to the water and push her in. Unable to swim, she would surely drown, and Shafia's problems with boyfriends and disobedience would be over.

The words he used to describe his daughter surprised and shocked Fazil. "Prostitute, whore — these are very bad words, ugly words in our culture," he told the court. "No one is using that against his own children. He just wanted to flare up my emotions and [make me] accept his request. He was very angry."

Fazil hung up on his brother-in-law. "I swore at him and I cut the line," he said. Then he tried to call his brother in Montreal to warn him that if he heard of any trips being planned, to "tell police he has such an intention." Ahmed wasn't home when Javid called with his warning. When Tooba phoned Sweden, Fazil told her about the plot her husband was hatching.

"I told her, Shafia wants to kill Zainab, to drown her. He told me he will put her in water and drown her. If he wants to take her on a trip, don't accept." Fazil told Tooba she should go to the police in Montreal, but she asked him no questions and made no commitments. "She told me it was very good you told me. Nothing else she said."

Fazil said the experience unnerved him so much he had to start seeing a psychiatrist. Asked at the trial why Shafia, who considered Fazil a sworn enemy, would suddenly try to enlist him in a plot to kill Zainab, he replied that his brother-in-law's reasoning was obvious.

"Everybody would have thought I would have been the main suspect. Today you would have seen me in that [prisoners'] box," he said. "One hundred percent, everybody would have thought I was the murderer."

The defence also asked why Shafia would murder Geeti when she, unlike her older sisters, wasn't seeing boyfriends. "Why did he kill Geeti? That's a very good question," Fazil said. "She [would be] a very good witness. She would be sitting here as a witness. She would be able to open up and tell all the secrets."

# The plan…

WHEN Hamed flew to Dubai on June 1, 2009, he had with him a black Champion-brand suitcase and his Toshiba laptop computer. Shafia had both an apartment in Dubai and an office that he shared with a business partner. The laptop was seized by Kingston Police in a raid on the Shafia home the night before Mohammad, Tooba, and Hamed were arrested and charged with the first-degree murders of their family members.

Constable Derek Frawley, a certified forensic computer analyst with the Kingston force, sifted through 278,000 entries on the laptop and found some unusual Google searches. On June 3, for example, someone had entered, in English: "can a prisoner have control over their real estate."

On June 13, Hamed and Mohammad returned home from Dubai. A number of other searches followed, such as "facts and documentaries on murders," and then, on June 20, "where to commit a murder." There was a Google map search centred on Middle Road and Highway 401 in Kingston, an area described by Frawley as being "right by the locks" — the locks at Kingston Mills.

The forensic work performed on the laptop by Kingston Police was one example of the complex high-tech case police were piecing together. Early in their investigation, police had gotten the cellphone numbers of all the family members, allowing Detective Steve Koopman to compile an exhaustive record of the calls and texts that went to and from the phones. On June 20, the day of the Google search for "where to commit a murder," Hamed's cellphone was activated in the Mont-Laurier, Quebec, region, the place where the Shafias would stay three days later.

Police were able to track the movements of the family on their Niagara Falls trip by the signals from the phones as they bounced off towers along their route. On June 24, Sahar's phone was pinging off the Station Road cell tower, just south of the lockstation, from 8:36 pm to 9:16 pm. By 9:23 pm, it was activated at the Centennial Drive cell tower several kilometres away in Kingston's west end. The family drove all the way to Niagara Falls that night, which would have put them there at around 1 am or later on June 25.

The Shafias stayed in Niagara Falls for four days. They didn't appear to do much other than check out the tourist sites, eat fast food, and go to a mall. There was, however, that one aberration. In the middle of the stay, on June 27, Hamed's phone is recorded at the Westbrook cellphone tower several kilometres west of Kingston.

At the trial, Shafia testified that he had decided to leave his family in Niagara Falls and head back to Montreal to complete some business. Police found it odd that Hamed's cellphone, which he claimed he always had with him, would have been with Shafia in the Lexus. Shafia said he, too, was surprised when it rang near Kingston. It was a call from his children saying they missed him, that they were becoming bored in Niagara, and that they wanted him to return — which he did, without ever getting to Montreal.

The police theory was much different. They suspected that Hamed and Shafia were both in the Lexus that day. The reason for their hasty trip: to scout out Kingston Mills, where they had stopped just three days before to use the washrooms, as a suitable place to commit a quadruple murder.

# The ruse...

KINGSTON Police asked Mohammad, Tooba, and Hamed to come to Kingston on July 18 to retrieve their belongings left in the Kingston East Motel room. The Shafias were also hoping to get their vehicles back — both the Lexus and the Nissan. This was all part of a ruse devised by police.

Once they suspected the three family members of murder, police applied for a warrant to plant listening devices in both the minivan and the home belonging to the Shafias. In Canada, it is both illegal and unconstitutional to intercept private communications using a wiretap without first obtaining a warrant through the court.

At the station, officers asked the Shafias to leave their van unlocked in case it had to be moved. They did so and went into the office. This gave police the time they needed to place a wiretap in the van.

For the next four days, the Shafias would be monitored and recorded from a police centre in Ottawa. Their conversations would be translated into English and carefully scrutinized by investigators. The recordings would provide some of the most damning evidence at trial: the now infamous words of Shafia, callings his daughters "whores," exhorting the devil to "shit on their graves," and vowing that if they ever returned to life, he would take a cleaver to them.

After turning over the belongings, police asked the Shafias if they wanted to go to Kingston Mills to see where their family members had died. They agreed, and the first stop, with the Shafias following the police in their van, was the Kingston East Motel. "We want to take you through what we think happened," a police officer's voice can be heard on the van wiretap. "So we think they [the Nissan] started [from] here, and then the locks are north from here."

Police, of course, didn't believe this version of events at all. They no longer accepted the Shafias' story that the four women were at the motel that night and left on a joyride to Kingston Mills. But they were willing to play along for now.

At Kingston Mills, the three Shafias walked around the grounds. Police then told them that one of the canal buildings had had a surveillance camera operating the night of June 29-30. Of course, this was not true; there was no camera. But the information had the effect police had hoped for.

Mohammad, Tooba, and Hamed were barely back in their van and on the highway when Hamed began talking about what the police had just told them.

"They're lying," Shafia told him. "If there was a camera, they'd access it in a minute." Tooba kept returning to the topic. "If there had been a camera, they would have taken it out a long time ago and checked it," she said. "They wouldn't have left it like that. They're just lying; they're trying to sound us out." Then, a few minutes later, she added: "There was no camera over there. I looked around; there wasn't any. If, God forbid, God forbid, there was one in that little house, all three of us [were there], no?"

Tooba then turned the conversation in another direction. "There was a lot of water, not a little ... There was a piece of wood. How come it didn't get stuck there?" she asked.

"That piece was far," her husband answered.

"God so took away their common sense, they didn't think they had no business there," Tooba said.

"God knows ... his works," Shafia replied. "That night there was no electricity there, everywhere was pitch darkness. You remember, Tooba?"

"Yes," she said.

"There wasn't the slightest glimmer of light or electricity," Shafia told her. "Even that room's light was off."

These conversations could be interpreted in different ways. But the detailed description Shafia provides Tooba — about the lack of electricity and the pitch darkness — would resonate with jurors at their trial.

"You remember, Tooba?" Shafia asked her directly. This was more than conjecture about what Kingston Mills might look like at night. He was sharing a statement of fact. The three were clearly preoccupied on their ride home to Montreal with the thought of a video camera being at the Mills, right down to discussing whether a device could record through a glass window or not.

Then Hamed had a realization: maybe they were being listened to at that moment.

"Right now, the car was at the police place; it was open," he told his parents. "They can fasten something to record your voice." By now, they saw Kingston Police as adversaries.

"They're keeping the car because they want to render a person's morale weak, do you understand, Tooba?" Mohammad said.

As they near home, Tooba rouses from a nap and tells the other two what she has been dreaming. "I just dozed off," she said. "Their boyfriends and all are wandering about, fit and happy. They've gone under ground."

"Damn on their boyfriends," Shafia replied. "To hell with them and their boyfriends ... filthy and rotten children."

The next day, July 19, the three were driving to see the big house Shafia was building in Brossard. They discussed which bedrooms the surviving children would take and where they would go to school. The children, other than Hamed, apparently didn't want to move. Shafia wondered if they would go to the child protection authorities "like [the] others." He said something unintelligible then, "This is so God's curse wouldn't be coming upon them like it did on the others."

They had a discussion about the oldest surviving daughter, who had assured her mother that she had never had a boyfriend.

"Tooba, they said the same thing," Shafia replied. Then he accused his other son of knowing about Ammar Wahid, the "Pakistani boy." "Would a son be like that? God's curse on such a son," said Shafia.

Tooba insisted that Zainab found Ammar of her own accord, without help from her youngest brother.

"No, Tooba, he spoke with the Pakistani just now," Shafia insisted. Then his anger turned toward Zainab. "Whatever she threw in our way, she did," said Shafia. "We lost our honour."

The issue now was how would they prevent the other children from following in the defiant, non-compliant footsteps of Zainab, Sahar, and Geeti. Hamed believed the move to another house and a new school would help.

"The important thing is that they are away from these friends and stay away from such friends," Hamed concluded.

But his father's ire was building. "Even if they come back to life a hundred times, if I have a cleaver in my hand, I will cut him/her in pieces," Shafia said. "Not once but a hundred times as they acted that cruel towards you and me. For the love of God, what had we done? What harm did we do to them? What excess had we committed, that they found to rear up and, as Iranians say, undressed themselves in front of boys? ... Every night I used to think of myself as a cuckold ...

"If we remain alive one night or one year, we have no tension in our hearts [thinking that] our daughter is in the arms of this or that boy, in the arms of this or that man. God curse their graduation! Curse of God on both of them, on their kind. God's curse on them for a generation! ... May the devil shit on their graves! Is that what a daughter should be? Would [she] be such a whore?"

At trial, the Crown showed a number of photos taken by Sahar and Zainab on their cellphone cameras of themselves wearing what could be either bathing suits or bras and panties. Sahar had also been photographed with Ricardo Sanchez, her boyfriend, and other young men, while she was wearing stylish modern clothes such as short shorts and low-cut tops.

Shafia was clearly upset that two of his surviving children knew about the photos. "Shameless girl with a bra and underwear," he said. "I swear to God that even those who do ads of such clothes are not like that. And these two others are hiding their photos."

Tooba reminded her husband that two of the surviving children had warned them that "we should be careful of their [Zainab and Sahar's] behaviour." The children were expected to report to their parents about their older siblings, in effect, acting as spies at school. There was, for example, the incident with the younger brother confronting Ricardo Sanchez at the restaurant and the deception he had to practise by kissing Sahar's friend.

Hamed had a plan: "We will pick them up from school and drop them back at school."

"Or," said his father, "if we feel that it is not working that way, we will move back to Dubai."

Police listening in on these conversations were no doubt concerned for the remaining children. If, as they suspected, it only took the perception of bad behaviour to get four family members killed, might it also happen to the others?

The next evening, July 20, another wiretapped conversation in the van had Shafia defending his relationship with his dead daughters, insisting he never meddled in their affairs. But he was clearly still obsessed with Zainab's behaviour. Tooba said he called her "filthy." Shafia insisted he would only have said that in relation to her "sinning and fornication."

"They're gone now. Shit on their graves," he concluded, hardly the words of a grieving man who'd lost three of his daughters just three weeks earlier.

Less than an hour later, the wiretap continued with this statement by Tooba: "I know Sadaf [Zainab] was already done, but I wish [the] two others weren't."

Shafia replied: "No, Tooba, they messed up. There was no other way ... No, Tooba, they were treacherous. They were treacherous. They betrayed both themselves and us ... For this reason, whenever I see those pictures, I am consoled. I say to myself, 'You did well. Would they come back to life a hundred times, for you to do the same again.' That is how hurt I am, Tooba. They betrayed us immensely. They violated us immensely."

The next night, Shafia continued telling himself he had done the right thing.

"Even if they hoist me up onto the gallows, nothing is more dear to me than my honour. Let's leave our destiny to God and may God never make me, you, or your mother honourless," he told Hamed. "I don't accept this dishonour ... Either you see them doing those bad things or hear that they did, but they did wrong."

Shafia was offended by his daughters' actions at a deeply personal level. "There is nothing more valuable than our honour," he said. "I am telling you now and I was telling you before that whoever play[s] with my honour, my [answer is] the same ... There is no value of life without honour."

If there was a Crown case to be made that the deaths of Rona, Zainab, Sahar, and Geeti were motivated by honour, it came from Mohammad Shafia's own words, repeated over and over on the wiretaps.

The photos Shafia ranted about would become a heavily contested matter at trial. When police raided the house on July 21, they found many of the pictures of Zainab, Sahar, and Rona in the suitcase Hamed had taken to Dubai to meet up with his father. It was the Crown's contention that these prompted Shafia to plot and carry out the honour killings of his children.

# The arrests...

O N the evening of July 21, Kingston Police arrived unannounced at 8644 rue Bonnivet with Montreal police officers and child protection workers.

Three of the surviving Shafia children were removed from the house and taken into protective care. Hamed, Tooba, and Mohammad were ordered out of the house while police conducted a search inside. They were told they were suspects in the murders of Rona, Zainab, Sahar, and Geeti. But police did not arrest them that night. Instead, with three of the younger children safely out of the house, they planted a listening device in the house telephone.

The next morning, a family friend picked up Hamed, Tooba, and Mohammad at their house. They were going to consult a lawyer about getting their children back. A Montreal police surveillance team was watching as they left the house and drove off. The Shafias never got to the lawyer's office. At a busy intersection, their vehicle was cut off and the arrests made. The three were taken to a Montreal police station, charged, then immediately transported to Kingston, three hours away.

# The interviews/
# interrogations...

WHEN they first appeared at Kingston Police headquarters on June 30, 2009, to report four family members missing, Mohammad Shafia, Tooba Mohammad Yahya, and their son Hamed Shafia had a simple story to tell. They arrived late in Kingston; Zainab borrowed the keys to the Nissan to get clothes from the trunk; and they woke up that morning to find the car and the four women gone.

All three were interviewed by police that afternoon, and officers noticed discrepancies in their stories. Later, when they were arrested on July 22 in Montreal and officially charged with the four murders, the interrogations that followed in Kingston highlighted more inconsistencies. The following are excerpts from both the June 30 interviews and July 22 and 23 interrogations.

### Mohammad...
Mohammad Shafia was interviewed by Detective Geoff Dempster starting around 3:45 pm on June 30. He told Dempster about the family trip to Niagara Falls and how they were heading home to Montreal in the early hours of June 30 when they decided to take a room at the Kingston East Motel.

At one point, said Shafia, "my wife said that [she is] very dizzy and cannot drive and will pull over somewhere. You guys get a hotel, eh, so we can go. We got here and this motel was expensive, too ... The motel is very expensive because we got tired and could no longer drive."

He told Dempster that they decide to go with the second motel they come across after exiting Highway 401. "Yes, at the second place, and we paid the money, and signed and everything. My wife was with the girls, these four people."

He said that the four women who later died went to room No. 18. Then Hamed announced he was going on to Montreal.

"Last night?" Dempster asked, during the June 30 interview.

"We got settled in, we got our place here," said Shafia, "and he said, I have to go, since tomorrow I have to work on the building or something, and, if necessary, then I will come back ... He was going alone because he had work and we didn't want to go. We wanted to stay for two or three nights. Right."

Dempster asked what happened next.

"Then, I woke up in the morning, uh, ... I saw that the car is not there," said Shafia.

After more questioning, however, Shafia said that initially it was he and Hamed and three of the younger children who went to the Kingston East Motel to sign in while Tooba waited in the Nissan with the four women further up Highway 15. Dempster also learned from the interview that while Hamed left for Montreal overnight in the Lexus, he returned to Kingston in the minivan. At 5 pm the interview ended.

Shafia was interrogated on July 23 by Royal Canadian Mounted Police inspector Shahin Mehdizadeh. An Iranian by birth,

Mehdizadeh was brought in from British Columbia to conduct the interviews with Shafia and Tooba in Farsi. By this time, Mehdizadeh had already spoken with Tooba and Hamed.

Early in the interview, Mehdizadeh asked Shafia why someone would want to kill his daughters. Shafia replied: "For us there wasn't any reason. For us they were pure and sinless kids. They were our children."

He then complained to the officer that someone had likely called the police to accuse him of killing Zainab. He told Mehdizadeh that it was probably her boyfriend, Ammar, who actually threatened to kill her. Mehdizadeh made it clear that police didn't believe the deaths were accidental.

"Someone has killed them," he said.

"Yes," replied Shafia.

"Someone has pushed them."

"This killer should be found," Shafia agreed.

Mehdizadeh confronted Shafia with the information from the cellphone records showing someone had travelled to the Kingston region on June 27 in the middle of the Niagara Falls vacation. The two went back and forth for several minutes as the officer tried to establish exactly who had gone where that day. Shafia admitted to nothing.

They turned to the events of the early morning hours of June 30 when the Nissan went into the water. "I, my son, my wife, I, all of us were in the motel," he insisted.

They talked about the situation with Zainab wanting to marry Ammar Wahid, then Shafia switched to Hussain Hyderi, the new fiancé.

"We would have given," he said of the second arrangement.

"We were very happy." Hardly the sentiment he expressed in the wiretaps.

Mehdizadeh asked who Rona was to him. "She is my cousin," Shafia replied. The officer showed him a picture of their wedding day.

"No, this is, it was, her birthday or something. This is not marriage. I haven't married her."

"Her family says that you had married her."

"No."

Mehdizadeh told Shafia they had wiretap recordings of him saying nasty things about his daughters. "You have been very upset with these girls," he suggested.

"No."

"I myself have heard it that you have said it," said the officer.

"No, [that] I might have said it. I never say such words [about] my daughter. I have said [about] my daughter, for example, that [going] to the water, she killed the other children. She has done a wrong thing," Shafia replied.

Mehdizadeh pondered why 13-year-old Geeti had to be killed.

"None of them had done anything," said Shafia.

Then Shafia was told about the pieces of headlight from Kingston Mills being matched up with the pieces found in the Lexus.

"It's impossible," Shafia said, not once, but twice.

Mehdizadeh warned Shafia that he wouldn't be able to go into court and continually deny the accusations and the evidence by just saying no over and over. When Mehdizadeh talked again about the wiretap evidence, Shafia told him he knew a device had been planted in their home.

"Today, even a child would know it that you have put something there. If he knows this, he wouldn't say these words. Is he talking these words so you can record them and come here and tell us?"

"You didn't know this," said the officer.

"These are childish words," Shafia told him. Then he insisted he even knew about the bug in the Pontiac van.

When Mehdizadeh accused him of beating his children, information gathered from the children and other people, Shafia continued to deny.

"The children are lying," he said. Then he pronounced his love for the dead women. "These four people have gone. [I] swear to God, I loved them with my heart. Alas, if I say these words, it isn't good. I wish God would have taken my life and spared their lives. I would have been ready ... I am not a criminal."

The interrogation ended in a heated exchange. "You are also a liar," said Mehdizadeh. "Your son is also a liar. The son is like the father."

"No," said Shafia.

"Both of you are dishonourable people."

"No."

"The honour of your family is in the hands of your women."

"No, you are not saying the right word," said Shafia.

## Tooba...

Tooba Mohammad Yahya does not come across as a typically submissive Afghan Muslim wife. A plain woman, she is not as pretty as her co-wife Rona, nor as compassionate. Stubborn and severe, she frequently frustrates her interrogators with her obstinacy. She is often sharp and sarcastic during questioning, critical of her husband

and excessively protective of her son Hamed. She shows little emotion for her three dead daughters.

Tooba was the last of the three to be interviewed by Dempster on June 30. Her account of the events of early that morning were slightly more detailed than her husband's.

"Me, very bad vomiting. I couldn't drive so I stopped the car," she said. "But my husband didn't know that I am vomiting. I said, myself, I will stop and you guys go ahead and get a motel and come get me. Me with [the] four [others]."

Tooba said she went directly to her room in the Kingston East Motel to sleep.

"Not too long after, my older daughter came and knocked on the door and asked for the keys to pick up some clothes from the car trunk," she said.

It was her husband who alerted her to the missing women and car the next morning.

She told Dempster about Zainab's being anxious to return to Montreal. Then, abruptly, she said: "Excuse, she told me a couple times [to] give [her] the keys, so [she] can drive. Give [her] keys to drive, but I didn't."

Tooba said she knew Hamed was going to Montreal that night, she thought for some business with the family's shopping plaza. She wasn't awake when he left. "If I knew I would have gone with him," she said. This despite being so sick in the car that the whole family had to pull over to stay in Kingston for the night.

Dempster asked Tooba what she thought happened with her daughters and Rona. She had already dropped the hint about Zainab's demanding to drive the car despite not having a licence.

"No matter how much I think, I don't know how they dared.

They left with the car," she said. "Always, always a girl who would [have her way]. She would do whatever she wanted to do."

In other words, Zainab was headstrong and taking the car would not be out of character.

Dempster asked again for a reason why they would have taken the car.

"Only desired, only desired to drive a car. She desired a lot. I think she thought, my mom and dad are asleep, let's go for a drive and return. That's it."

Dempster then left the interview room and returned with another question for Tooba. "Were you there when the car went in the water?" he asked.

"I was not there. [After] they got the key from me I didn't know anything," she replied.

Dempster tried to determine where Hamed was at the time Zainab supposedly came for the car keys. Tooba suggested Hamed and Shafia heard the Nissan drive away. Then, after further questioning, she backed away from this notion and said, "We didn't know that they were gone at that time," adding that everyone assumed the girls had gone to their rooms.

This didn't make sense, of course, because if Hamed then left for Montreal, he would have known the Nissan was already missing. Dempster then suggested that Hamed got in the Lexus and went after the girls. Tooba said she didn't know anything about this because she was so tired.

Tooba's interrogation on July 22 with Shahin Mehdizadeh of the RCMP was far more intense. It began at 5:31 pm and did not end until nearly 1 am the next morning. Mehdizadeh told Tooba that they no longer needed to discuss how the deaths took place, only why the Shafias carried out the murders.

The officer showed Tooba a picture of Kingston Mills and asked if she could remember stopping there on the way to Niagara Falls. She said they did not. He asked about June 27 and whether Mohammad or Hamed left the family in Niagara Falls at that time. At first she said no, then recalled Mohammad's being gone and that he had likely taken Hamed's cellphone with him.

Mehdizadeh asked her to talk about her daughters, particularly Zainab.

"The girls were good girls," she said, "but the problem was between Zainab that I have already mentioned. She, Zainab, loved a Pakstani boy and he also said that he loved her. They had asked us [for] her hand in marriage, too."

Tooba recounted the botched marriage and the annulment and the pressures that fell on her. Zainab's insistence on marrying appeared to be the breaking point for Tooba, borne out in the court testimony provided by her brother, Fazil. She described Mohammad as a good provider who spent money on his children, "but he is not so attached to them." She insisted that he never hit them, then relented, saying he did sometimes.

They moved on to discuss Rona. Mehdizadeh asked about her relationship to Mohammad.

"She is the daughter of my husband's uncle," Tooba said evasively. "I was 17 years old when I married him. I ... Rona was ... Rona was there, but as his uncle's daughter. When I was asking, he was saying, 'my uncle's daughter,' but I haven't noticed anything that she had something with him."

This, of course, was an incredible statement to make. She insisted that after 20 years of being married to Shafia, she knew noth-

117

ing about his marriage to Rona, though Rona was at their wedding and was living in their home.

"When I came, he was single," she said.

More than two hours into the interrogation, Mehdizadeh explained how the Nissan could not have fallen over the edge of the canal without being pushed in. "Do you think that this is still an accident now?" he asked. "This is murder. Whoever had done this, he did it to kill them. Do you agree or not?"

Tooba said, "No, this is right; what you are saying is right." She insisted Shafia never told her about a plot to kill the children. "If he had told me that he would kill the children, especially Zainab, I would go to the police with my children," she said. "Believe me, I would have done this."

Mehdizadeh showed Tooba a series of photos of the Lexus headlight reconstruction and told her that the damage matched with the rear of the Nissan.

Tooba picked up the narrative: "...Now the important thing is to specify the person — who was that person who hit it with the other car, pushed it into the water ... This is important, isn't it?"

Mehdizadeh agreed, suggesting it was Hamed, because he later took the Lexus to Montreal.

"No," she insisted, "before it [the Lexus] was with his Dad ... before it was with his dad ... they were changing [cars]." Then later she said, "... It is very important to specify at that moment, who was in that car. This is more important in my view."

"This was 2 o'clock," said Mehdizadeh.

"You are saying right," Tooba replied.

Slowly but surely the officer was gathering key information. Mehdizadeh told her about the van wiretaps and how she had already incriminated herself, placing them at Kingston Mills prior to the deaths.

"I am certain you have been there," he said.

"No, never," Tooba replied.

Then he pointed out how ludicrous it would be for Rona, more than 50 years old, to go on a joyride at 2 o'clock in the morning. "That woman was 50 years old but you would have thought she was a 25-year-old girl," Tooba responded.

Tooba then admitted in the video interrogation that one of her brothers had told her about Shafia's saying he wanted to kill Zainab. "He had told my brother, yes," she said, but he never said anything directly to her. "My brother told me that he had told [him] this, so it's obvious that he has done it then, maybe," Tooba said.

Then there was a breakthrough. Tooba placed herself at Kingston Mills that night, sitting in the car with the four women and waiting for her husband and Hamed to return from finding a motel room.

"But I request you one thing that [you] never tell my husband," she said. "Yes, never tell my husband that I have said this."

At one point, she said Zainab needed to go to the washroom. "We got out and wanted to go to the toilet. Since it was dark, she got scared. She was scared and said, No, I don't want to go. Wait till Dad comes.' When her dad ... uh, while the car was parked on this side at the corner of the street ... when her dad came, I went and sat with the two. But her dad was behind the wheel, behind the Lexus was her dad. I went and sat with him. Once I sat with him, believe me that I don't know anything what had happened since then."

She claimed she fell asleep in the Lexus but then described a scene that police believe may have occurred — some form of pre-drowning of the women at the basin below the top lock.

"If I was awake," she said, "and they were pressing and putting them into the water, I might have known it. As a human, I would have been shaken or would have heard a sound of splashing or something, but that time, believe me, I don't know nothing about the detail of this story how it has happened."

She appeared to be telling the story of the deaths, cautiously, without implicating herself.

"Did these girls, did these girls ever come into the motel? Did this car ever come to the motel?" Mehdizadeh asked. "Tell me the truth."

"No. I told you no," said Tooba.

"This car has never come to the motel?"

"No."

On a piece of paper, Mehdizadeh drew Kingston Mills and the location of the cars for her to see.

"What were these girls doing? Madam, what am I saying? I am telling you that when someone falls into the cold water, it is not a joke to say that I fell into this cold water. It is not a joke to say that I fell into this cold water. I am suffocated and will die ... Were those ladies asleep or awake? Tell me the truth."

Tooba: "Let me think about it. No, they were awake. They were awake."

Mehdizadeh: "So you are saying they were awake. Somebody came and took the car from there to here and pushed it in and nobody, nobody, uh, all of them were sitting in the car to die?... I am not [a] stupid person!"

"No, your claim is right," she said.

He implored her, in the memory of her dead daughters, to

tell him the truth. They went over the story again about who was driving which vehicle at the locks.

"When we changed the car and they went, I was with the girls, sitting calmly," Tooba began again. "My older daughter said she wanted toilet, then we got off and saw it was dark."

Mehdizadeh was growing impatient again. "You have told me this," he said.

Tooba picked up the story when the Lexus returned to the lockstation and she ran to it. "Both of them came out of Lexus," Tooba said. "Shafia was driving. Yes, then Hamed was standing there. I don't know whether he was peeing or doing something else. Anyway, he was standing on the other side. Then I came and Shafia took the Lexus. Shafia took the Lexus."

She went on: "He came and I was standing with Hamed on the other side talking with him. I was talking with him and I heard a sound. [Do] you understand? But I ask you not to tell Shafia about this. Believe me, don't tell Shafia. I heard a noise. Hamed and I heard it. We both ran and we saw a car was in the water. This car had fallen into the water."

Tooba acknowledged the Lexus was also at the edge of the lock where the Nissan fell in.

Mehdizadeh wanted to know how the vehicles got there. "Who, who brought the car, the Nissan, from where you were waiting for them when Shafia and Hamed came? Who brought this car to the place where it fell into the water? Who was driving? Were you driving or Shafia?" he demanded.

"Shafia," Tooba replied.

"Or Hamed?"

"Shafia was driving."

121

Then came this almost inconceivable recount by Tooba of her daughters' last moments: "I, I just, just saw that, when the noise came from the water, since Hamed and I was a bit far away. Hamed was walking around and we were chatting ... When the noise of the water came, I, when the noise of the water came, we ran. We ran and came [to the water]. We came. At that moment I became so stressed, as I didn't understand where the Lexus was or where this car was ..."

Mehdizadeh asked: "What were the girls doing when the car went into the water?"

"Nothing," she replied. "I, believe me, I fell down. I screamed and fell down ... I screamed and fell down so I didn't understand that this car — where the Lexus went — what happened to this car? Just when I realized [the Nissan] went into the water, I screamed and fell down. I screamed and fell down so ... I became unconscious.

"Hamed and I ran. We ran and we saw that the car was in the water. After that, I don't remember. Believe in God that I didn't understand anything. I grab my hair and fell down, fell down, then I didn't understand."

Then: "When I got to the motel, I was still not thinking that the girls had fallen into the water. I thought that their dad had already taken them. I was thinking like this. Do you understand?"

"No," said Mehdizadeh, "It's impossible because you knew that the girls were in the car."

"They were in the car," she agreed, "but I was thinking this: Why [didn't] these girls come down after me because they were always coming after me. Wherever I was going, they were following me. I was thinking like the car had been fallen empty."

Tooba said Shafia drove to the Kingston East Motel and Hamed helped her into the room. But Mehdizadeh went back to the scene at Kingston Mills.

"You saw Shafia was driving and hit at the back of this car with the Lexus and pushed it into the water?" he asked.

"I didn't see it [with] my eyes," said Tooba. "Didn't see it with my eyes — just I am telling [you] that I didn't see the Lexus with my eyes pushing the other. Believe me, I didn't see this with my eyes."

After she screamed and fell down, Mehdizadeh wanted to know, did Hamed try to help his sisters? "Hamed went into the water to save them?" he asked.

"Into the water, no. He couldn't go into the water."

"Why?" Mehdizadeh asked.

"He couldn't go [because] we ran and I fell down."

"Nobody called the police?"

"To the police?" said Tooba. "I don't know anything after that. I don't know anything."

Mehdizadeh pointed out how perplexing the family's actions were from that point on. Hamed drove to Montreal, ostensibly for business or to get the laptop and didn't report the incident from that night. The rest of them went to bed at the Kingston East Motel and didn't call police.

"Shafia was there. You say that Shafia has done this. Okay, obviously Shafia didn't want to call the police," said Mehdizadeh. "What else [did] he want to do, because you said Shafia was behind the wheel of the Lexus. Their mother is there. Their brother is there. A brother who, when the Lexus hits a pole in Montreal the next day, immediately calls the police because of the accident. Nobody called the police here."

Tooba's response was to defend Hamed. "Maybe he didn't have his cellphone," she offered.

"No, it was with him," said Mehdizadeh. He pulled out all the stops, taking Tooba's hands in his, begging for the truth so the victims could rest peacefully in their graves. Later, in the courtroom, Mohammad and Tooba both broke down crying. On the video screen, Tooba began to backtrack from her statements. Mehdizadeh again wanted to know what the women were doing as the car went over the edge.

"How do I know that?" she replied with one of the most chilling remarks of the entire trial. "In the darkness, it was as dark as the grave over there."

Realizing she had told too much, Tooba's story started to change. When she and Hamed heard the car go into the water, she thought Shafia had moved the children from the Nissan to the Lexus. But why, Mehdizadeh asked, would Shafia plunge the Nissan into the water?

"I didn't know whether the children were [in it] or not," she said. "I didn't know anything. I became unconscious."

Mehdizadeh clenched his fists in front of him and asked Tooba: "Do you see that their hands are like this? Do you know why they became like this? Because they have been drowned, Madam. You are trying to tell me that no one, none of them, wanted to come out of the car?"

They argued over why neither she nor Hamed called the police. Tooba said it was because she was unconscious. Why not Hamed, then? "Maybe he also became unconscious," said Tooba.

Mehdizadeh continued to press her to tell him why she helped kill her daughters.

"I didn't have any reason and didn't help [with] this. In fact, I didn't help Shafia in killing them, believe me," she said calmly. Now, several hours into the investigation, Tooba decided to push back. "You said I helped," she said. "Do you have any evidence that I have helped them?"

Mehdizadeh showed her a photo of Geeti drowned in the car. Her hand, he said, was pointing toward Sahar's in the back seat, as if she were reaching out to the sister she loved so much. "At least have a little respect for your daughters. Their graves are still cold. Their graves haven't even warmed up yet," he said.

Instead of breaking down under the continued pressure from Mehdizadeh, Tooba got more confident. She wanted Mehdizadeh to say why he thought the girls didn't try to escape from the car. "Tell me your thoughts why these girls [didn't] come out," she said, insisting that she didn't know herself. "If they were unconscious — all those medical examinations have been completed ... The medical test has been conducted, right? So why hasn't it shown [anywhere] that they had been unconscious?"

Mehdizadeh said the autopsy wasn't completed. Then he cut to the chase. "Have you killed them," he asked.

"No."

"Shafia has killed them?"

"No, I don't know."

"Nobody?"

"I don't know what has happened. What has happened, I don't know myself, don't know," said Tooba. "Somebody else has killed them."

The next day, she informed police that she was recanting everything she'd told Mehdizadeh during the interrogation.

**Hamed...**

Hamed Shafia, the second child and first son of Mohammad Shafia and Tooba Mohammad Yahya, appears sullen and angry in photographs and on the videotape. He is a good-looking young man but not handsome, bearing a strong resemblance to his mother. He is quiet, his emotions seemingly held in check, and speaks in an understated monotone when questioned. Like his mother, he frequently contradicts himself, compounding one lie with another.

Hamed was interviewed twice on June 30, 2009, by Detective Geoff Dempster at the Kingston Police station. In the afternoon interview, Dempster asked Hamed why he left for Montreal in the middle of the night.

"I needed something personal," Hamed answered vaguely. Later he told Dempster it was to retrieve his laptop which he had forgotten in Montreal, and had been without for a week. "There was a million reasons why I went there," he finally said.

He also slipped in information several times about Zainab and his sisters wanting to drive the car as a possible reason for their going on a joyride in the middle of the night. He recalled being "scared" watching Zainab drive in a parking lot. Even 13-year-old Geeti tried to drive, Hamed told Dempster. He admitted, however, that Rona's presence in the car didn't make sense.

"She was a person who really thought twice about doing things."

Dempster also wanted to know why Hamed went to Montreal in the Lexus but returned in the Montana minivan.

"That was my choice. I just thought I'd bring it," he explained.

Dempster told Hamed that someone at the locks overnight

heard a splash and that someone else saw a vehicle drive away from the scene.

"You mean someone pushed them in?" Hamed asked.

"No, that there was someone there," said Dempster.

Kingston Police then learned from Montreal police that Hamed had reported an accident that morning with the Lexus SUV in a supermarket parking lot. They decided to bring him in for another interview at 8:40 pm. Dempster asked him why he was hiding information. Why didn't he tell him about the accident earlier in the day?

"It was nothing related to this," Hamed said, referring to his sisters' deaths.

Dempster wanted to know why the women would have gone joyriding in the Nissan at such a late hour.

"I think they wanted to take it for a test drive," he replied.

Dempster was persistent. "It's weird," he told Hamed. "No one here can make any sense of it."

Hamed said he was in the motel room when Zainab asked for the keys to the Nissan. He then left for Montreal. The girls also left. He didn't know how they got from the motel to the bottom of the Rideau Canal.

"I have nothing to put on the table," Hamed told the officer.

At 11:25 pm on July 22, about 12 hours after being arrested in Montreal, Hamed was brought to an interrogation at the Kingston Police station to meet with Detective Steve Koopman. Koopman's assignment, early in the case, had been to befriend and develop a rapport with the family. He had been the one to escort the grieving parents to the morgue to identify the bodies. He also attended the funeral in Montreal on July 5 — by which time police had concluded

127

that the Lexus SUV had been used to push the Nissan into the canal.

Koopman zeroed in on the early morning of June 30 when the Shafias exited at Kingston to find a motel for the night. He established once again that Hamed and his father drove away in the Lexus to find a place and that they had three of his younger siblings with them.

Koopman: "Did they park on the side of a road? Did they park in a parking lot? Were they ..."

Hamed: "It was, it was in a parking lot, I think. Yeah." He told Koopman that after he and his father checked into the Kingston East, they went back up the road to find his mother and sisters and Rona. But the Nissan was already driving toward them. Hamed couldn't explain how this happened.

Hamed said he was only at the motel five or ten minutes when he decided to leave for Montreal. Mainly he wanted to check on a "building" they owned in the city.

"So how long were you in Montreal before the Lexus hit the rail?" Koopman asked.

"I went home, then, uh, when I had to eat something, I went and got up," he replied. "So if it was five ... If I got there at, like, six or five, maybe. Three hours, yeah, five-thirty, six. Then about two hours, I guess."

"OK," said Koopman, "So why wouldn't you have taken the Nissan back to Montreal?"

We don't hear Hamed's response because of a technical problem with the videotaping. Hamed was again asked about the accident with the Lexus in the Montreal supermarket parking lot. Koopman wanted to know how the pieces of Lexus headlight ended up inside the vehicle. Hamed said the Montreal police officer told him to collect them.

It was a meandering interview with Hamed always suggesting Koopman check the cellphone records to more accurately gauge where he was at different times.

"I guess in terms of where we are tonight and why you're sitting here, I just gotta ask, should I believe everything that you've told me tonight?" Koopman said.

"Yeah," Hamed replied. "If it wasn't the truth, I wouldn't tell you, but then if, uh, if you're saying, uh, if you're asking me, like, uh, asking me if you believe me or not, then, you know, it's up to you."

Koopman offered Hamed a chance to tell him anything else he might remember from the night and following morning of June 29-30. Hamed suggested that if Koopman were to give him more of the evidence against them that he could then "correct your mistake."

Koopman excused himself from the room then returned a short while later. He had been conferring with other officers watching the interview. He told Hamed that they had just given him new information and that he was not asking Hamed any longer if he and his parents killed the women — he wanted to know why they did it. Hamed didn't answer. Koopman asked Hamed if his father exerted control over him to help with the murders.

"It's not a question of did it happen, Hamed," said Koopman. "It's a question of why did it go that far?"

Hamed asked for more proof of their guilt. Koopman listed off all the lies he'd caught him in, such as supposedly having stayed in Niagara Falls all five days even though his cell phone registered off a tower near Kingston on June 27. Then he went over the fact that pieces of plastic from the Lexus headlight were found at the lockstation.

"I know," Hamed replied. "I understand that and I know ...

How are you involving the other two with me?... My question to you is how come my, uh, parents got into this?" Hamed told Koopman that his mother had "nothing to do with it 'cause she was not herself that night. She was really tired. She had no idea where we are and everything."

Koopman told him that she had just told police she heard the splash, "and she's admitting to us that she's seen the car in the water."

"I don't know," Hamed responded. "I don't know about that." He asked Koopman if he could meet with his mother. The officer said no. Hamed said he was perplexed that police could assume all three were involved in a murder if there was no video footage to prove it.

Koopman cut to the chase, telling him to forget about all the other details and tell him why pieces of the Lexus headlight were found at Kingston Mills.

"I don't know," Hamed answered.

"You do know that," said Koopman. "That's an absolutely horrible answer to give to me." He accused Hamed of staging the accident in Montreal to cover up the damage from using the Lexus to bump the Nissan into the locks. He told Hamed that the pieces of plastic were recovered the morning the car was discovered underwater.

Hamed again wanted to know when they were collected.

"What does it matter?" Koopman asked him. Hamed said members of Hussain Hyderi's family had visited Kingston and could have dropped the pieces in the grass. Koopman said again the pieces were collected the morning of June 30 by police when the area was sealed off from the public.

"That piece of [the] Lexus was there because you were there with that vehicle," Koopman said.

Hamed sputtered, saying he had no hope in his life and that "now it's your turn to answer my question."

Koopman corrected him. "You're not in a position to start demanding answers from me," he said. Then he told Hamed how disappointed he was in him.

"Listen, Steve, man," Hamed said, "uh, you know, and I understand what you said. You're, like, this is a serious situation, of course. It's murder. It should be serious for everyone." Hamed suggested police were only acting on information given them by accusing family members.

Koopman said they didn't make arrests based on people's opinions. He accused Hamed of dishonouring his sisters by not telling the truth. Then he left the interview room and Detective Sergeant Mike Boyles, who had been watching the interview, entered the room. He told Hamed he'd been lying to Koopman the whole time and that his mother, meanwhile, had been telling the truth.

"If your mom says all three of you were at the locks ... on the night ... if she told us you were all there, would that be a lie or the truth?" asked Boyles.

"I don't believe that my mom says this," Hamed replied.

"Well, I'm telling you she said that. I witnessed it with my own eyes," said Boyles.

"Well, if she was there, I don't know, but I wasn't."

Boyles became more assertive, telling Hamed that if he couldn't explain why his phone was in the Kingston area on June 27 in the middle of the vacation, then, "That's your story. That's just perfect." Police would take the information to trial.

Boyles switched to the headlight pieces found at the locks. "Was the headlight smashed when you left at two in the morning?" he asked.

"Uh, just forget about ..." said Hamed.

Boyles told Hamed they had been listening to the family's conversations on wiretaps for the past several days.

"Seriously," said Hamed, "you have no idea what you're saying."

Hamed looked at the photographs Boyles had put on the table and became entranced by those showing two of his dead sisters. Boyles asked him again to tell the truth.

"They're your family there, your blood," he said. "And I know, I know they weren't respecting the culture and they weren't respecting tradition."

"No, it was nothing like that," Hamed replied.

Boyles reminded Hamed of all the wiretapped conversations in the van. "These aren't conversations of innocent people," said Boyles. "You guys aren't mastermind criminals, Hamed, do you understand that? You guys aren't hitmen. You guys don't know how to cover your tracks properly. You don't know how to get away with things."

Boyles asked Hamed if he knew anyone who would want to kill his sisters. Hamed said no.

"What do you think happened to them?"

"What I guessed in the first place," said Hamed.

"What was that?"

"Taking the keys and driving," he replied. Hamed continued looking at the photos of his dead sisters after they were taken out of the car, seemingly mesmerized by them.

"Drowning is not a peaceful death, Hamed. Drowning is a horrible way to die. You understand that? It's a horrible way," Boyles said.

Hamed kept saying he wanted to leave. Boyles told him to wait, that they were finding the segment of Tooba's interrogation where she placed all three of them at Kingston Mills the night of the deaths.

During the trial, the courtoom was transfixed by the exchange between this young man and Boyles, the experienced detective who had come in as the "bad cop" to Steve Koopman's "good cop." The pressure on Hamed was intense. Yet he remained defiant. Then, the hushed courtroom watched the video as Boyles took another tack.

"I'm not going to ask you any more questions or anything," he said, "but I want you to know that at some point you're gonna go to trial and you're gonna be in court. And there's gonna be a jury or a judge who's gonna assess what happened ... So I guess if you want to just look at the camera, you can look right there and see it — you can't really see it, but it's right there. And you can talk to the jury and you can talk to the judge that'll see this in a year and a half. And you can say your piece and tell them what you think and how you feel. This is your opportunity because you're not gonna get another one. The next time, you'll be in the box and it will be at trial."

Two years and three months later, Hamed would be sitting in the prisoners' box in the courtroom, between his co-accused mother and father, watching Boyles predict the future on the video.

"Whatever I have, I tell in front of the judge at that time," Hamed told his interrogator. But he never did.

133

# Jailhouse confession...

OF all the strange twists and turns the Kingston Mills murder investigation and trial took, none was stranger — or more of a game changer — than the appearance of Moosa Hadi. Hadi was a young man of Afghan origin, studying mining engineering at Queen's University, when he took an interest in the Shafia case. He offered his translation services to Peter Kemp, Mohammad Shafia's defence lawyer from Kingston, not long after the arrests in the summer of 2009. Soon he was doing much more than that. Hadi began visiting Mohammad Shafia at the Quinte Detention Centre where the three accused were being held.

After speaking with Shafia, as well as Tooba, Hadi became convinced that this seemingly devout Muslim man would never hatch a plot to kill his daughters. Although Hadi had been hired by Shafia's lawyer to act as translator, Mohammad Shafia subsequently hired Hadi himself and paid him $4,500 to conduct his own investigation. Hadi asked permission to have access to all the police and Crown evidence to that point in the investigation, in particular the interviews and interrogations with police and the wiretaps — a seemingly outrageous request from someone with no qualifications, but Hadi was handed all the files. This in turn gave Shafia access to the Crown's evidence against him and his family.

Obsessed with his investigation, Hadi came to the conclusion that police were being given the wrong interpretations of the Shafias' statements and their surreptitiously taped conversations. He felt the Crown's case was biased and he convinced Shafia he could help correct this terrible injustice.

On November 7, 2009, Hadi visited Hamed at Quinte. He brought along his laptop computer to record their conversation. "I want to record the things that we are talking about. They will be recorded but they will remain with me only," Hadi says in the interview. They didn't.

Hadi decided that what Hamed told him that day was so favourable to the Shafias' case that police should hear it, too. On November 16, Hadi and his recording appeared in court — not as a witness for Hamed and his parents, but for the Crown, which had subpoenaed him to testify. His testimony and evidence would prove to be more beneficial to the Crown case.

For the first half of the three-hour interview at Quinte, Hadi did most of the talking, disputing the entire case constructed by the police and Crown attorneys. In the wiretaps, for instance, when Shafia was railing against his daughters, Hadi told Hamed that his father was not actually angry with the girls, but angry at their actions. He accused the RCMP's Shahin Mehdizadeh — "this stupid officer," he called him — of bullying Tooba during her interrogation. Hadi played segments of the interrogation for Hamed and analyzed them one by one.

Moosa Hadi proclaimed Hamed to be "100% innocent. The only sin that Hamed has is that after the incident or accident he hasn't declare[d] the truth."

Hamed began to tell his new-found ally a different version of what happened in the early hours of June 30. Hamed said they all drove to the Kingston East Motel that night but, of the four passengers in the Nissan, only Rona went inside. He claimed Geeti was asleep in the car; Zainab and Sahar were awake. Zainab and Sahar were sitting in the Nissan in the parking lot and they turned on the radio. Hamed was sitting next to them in the Lexus. Zainab told him she wanted to "drive the car and just go for a spin" in the parking lot.

"Before this, I think Rona wanted to buy a card to make some phone calls or something, so she also got in the car. She told me that if you want to go, before you go, bring me a card," Hamed recounted. Hamed told Rona that the stores were all closed that time of night. What did Rona do? She insisted they go look for a phone card, even though it was at least 1:30 in the morning and none of the women had a driver's licence. (In his original interview with police, Hamed had said Rona's presence in the Nissan didn't make sense. He said: "She was a person who really thought twice about doing things.")

Hamed said he wanted to get his mother so she could drive them for the phone card. Tooba, of course, was the reason they had stopped in Kingston, claiming to be seriously nauseous and vomiting. Yet Hamed claimed he was going to wake her up to go driving for a phone card in the middle of the night.

Their parents were already asleep, however, so Hamed decided to "let them go by themselves. Yes. After that, when I came, I saw that they had already started the car. So I said, I will go with you for a little distance.' I said, Be careful, I know you haven't driven much. Pay attention not to hit anything. Drive slowly, slowly, I will be following you.'"

In this new scenario, the Nissan headed onto Highway 15 and went north toward Highway 401, also in the direction of Kingston Mills, with Hamed following in the Lexus. They crossed over

Highway 401 and stopped at one of the gas stations at the hamlet of Codes Corners. Hamed pulled up beside them and told them he knew it would be closed. He urged them to turn back to the motel. But they didn't. Instead, Zainab took the car onto the Kingston Mills Road and Hamed followed again.

At the Mills, said Hamed, "I hit the back [of the Nissan] but not hard, just the glass was broken, the glass of Lexus car." He described a scene of some confusion with the occupants of the Nissan saying they would try to make a U-turn to head back where they had come from. They got stuck. Then "she," one of the women in the Nissan, told Hamed she couldn't make the turn.

Hamed and Hadi drew a map to indicate precisely where everyone was located. "Yeah, here or somewhere like this, I saw them for the last time," he said. "Before this, my mind was occupied over the damage."

By this time, Hamed claimed he was out of the Lexus, picking up pieces of broken headlight from the road.

"Yes. I had them in my hand when I heard the splash."

Hamed said he went to where he could still see a glow from the Nissan's headlights underwater — even though the evidence showed that when the car was found, the engine was turned off and so were the headlights. He said he put the pieces of headlight down near the lock "then went to get a rope ... I took it from the car and wanted to go inside to [get] them out."

By now, Hamed was familiar with all the police evidence, particularly their interview with a young boy who happened to be out on the deck of his house that night.

"Yeah, yeah, before that, the boy says, I heard a horn sound' right?" he asked Hadi. "I sounded the horn a bit to see if there was

137

anyone ... He says that he heard it for five seconds. I sounded it once. I realized that there was nobody there." Hadi asked again how many times he sounded the horn, as if prompting him to change his answer.

"Yeah. Twice, twice I did once, twice," he now said. "The area looked like a forest. It was very dark. I couldn't see through very well so I came here. When I came here I ... thought when I sounded the horn, [I] wished someone [would] come, or my sister who, if she is out of the car [i.e., not in the car], comes ... One of them was out of the car ... When I came and sat here, I put the rope but could not see anything."

Hamed's recollections became confusing at this point. "One of them got out," he said. Hadi asked which sister got out of the car. "I think it was Sahar. Sahar got out once."

This appeared to be a reference to some action prior to the car's going into the water. That, he said, was why he was thinking Sahar was not in the car. Hadi asked who was driving when the Nissan went into the water. Zainab was driving at first, Hamed said, but she may have switched with Sahar.

"They rolled the window down a bit, rolled down the window a bit," Hamed said, possibly in an effort to include that piece of known evidence in his testimony. Now he was more convinced that Sahar was driving the car when it went into the water.

Police would later reveal that Geeti was closest to the driver's seat with Zainab beside her in the front. Sahar was in the back with Rona.

"She switched with her," Hamed continued. "When I heard the sound there, I left all those and came here and sounded [the] horn a couple of times, and no one was there so I went back. I put the rope a few times in the water."

"Okay," prompted Hadi. "You put the rope into the water?"

"I put it into the water. Nothing happened ... I fold[ed] the rope back where [I] put it ... I fold and came back ... this way, came back and sat in the car." He said he called helplessly from atop the lock "but they were not responding."

"You were probably shaking the rope as well?" Hadi suggested, clearly prompting Hamed again.

"Yes, it was like that," agreed Hamed. "I moved it a little bit to see if they take it."

Despite the confusion and unfolding tragedy, Hamed also managed to go "back to the car with those pieces" of headlight he had set down at the side of the lock. Hamed estimated the time from when he heard the splash to when he went to sit in the Lexus to be 15 minutes.

"Okay, then you got back to the Lexus car," Hadi continued.

"Yes," said Hamed, "and then drove towards Montreal."

Then Hadi moved into damage control with his questioning, asking Hamed if at this point he thought about calling police to report what had happened. Yes, he thought about it, but decided not to.

"First, I thought that if I call the police, they would blame me that she didn't have a licence and [I had] brought her here," he said. Hamed said he drove away, then stopped briefly to think.

"I was thinking to call someone to come and help them, to come and help them. Nothing else came to my mind, such as ..."

"Like you will be charged with murder," Hadi interjected, again prompting Hamed.

"Yes, yeah. Just to find someone to give them help, but when I realized that [a] few minutes had passed, I was scared, so [I] turned the car and went towards Montreal."

As the interview continued, Hamed also had an explanation for the shards of headlight found at the lockstation. He dropped some of them in the confusion. Arriving in Montreal, Hamed said he was tortured about what to tell his parents. He admitted taking the Lexus to the supermarket lot to fake an accident. Then he received two phone calls from his father in Kingston, the second one informing him that the Nissan and the women were not at the motel.

When Hamed finally decided to tell his parents what really happened that night "there wasn't any opportunity to inform them." Hamed said he was worried about his father's reaction. "He might have become very upset," he said. "He would have sworn. He would have lost his temper badly as why they have gone with the car without permission."

Hamed decided to withhold his information and "disclose it to the judge" when they went to trial.

"Okay, so what made you say it now?" Hadi asked.

"Because you told me that now it's the time and don't waste the time of the court," said Hamed.

Hadi said that withholding this information from his parents caused them to suffer greatly in jail, accused of multiple murders, while his younger siblings were placed in protection. He urged Hamed to tell the truth about what really happened.

"I will talk with the lawyer and tell him the story," said Hamed. "I will tell him that to tell the Crown, too."

Hadi was relieved, believing Hamed's story would exonerate him. He hoped, in fact, that their conversation was being recorded by jail authorities. If not, he said, "I will reveal it." Which he did to Kingston Police when he turned over recordings of the conversation.

# The trial...

JURY selection for the Kingston Mills murder trial began on the morning of October 11, 2011. Ontario Superior Court Justice Robert Maranger had been selected as the presiding judge. Maranger, with his attention to detail, patience, and good humour, would turn out to be the perfect choice to guide this complicated trial.

Canadian jury trials require 12 jurors, as well as two alternates who are dismissed once the trial begins. The 14th and final person was selected on the afternoon of October 13 — seven men and seven women — as the three accused watched the Canadian justice system unfold from their seats in the glass prisoners' box.

The Crown attorneys on the case, Laurie Lacelle and Gerard Laarhuis, signalled loud and clear that while this was a quadruple murder trial — with Tooba Mohammad Yahya, Mohammad Shafia, and Hamed Shafia each charged with four counts of murder — the killings were motivated by honour based on cultural influences the elder Shafias had brought with them from the Greater Middle East.

Each of the accused had their own lawyer. Mohammad Shafia would be represented by Kingston attorney Peter Kemp. Tooba had also selected a Kingston lawyer, David Crowe. Several months before the trial began, Hamed changed lawyers, hiring Patrick McCann from Ottawa.

During pre-trial motions, McCann would take exception to

the Crown's plan to call University of Toronto professor Shahrzad Mojab as an expert on Middle Eastern honour killings. The Crown had crucial evidence from the wiretaps in the family van in which Shafia calls his daughters "whores," declaring that "there is no value in life without honour." The Crown needed someone like Mojab to help put the remarks into cultural context — essentially to show that the family's honour had been stained by the girls' relationships with boys, and that they had to be killed to cleanse that dishonour. In the end, Maranger allowed Mojab to testify.

Other ground rules were established for the coming months of the trial. Media were not to transmit stories from the courtroom using social media. The identities of the three surviving children and their images were not to appear in any stories or broadcasts. And at one point in the proceedings, the entire court would be transported to Kingston Mills so the jurors could see firsthand the place where the bodies were discovered and where the Crown alleged an appalling set of murders had been committed.

Daily workings of the court depended on the smooth running of the translation services. Each day, three interpreters at the trial translated from Farsi to English and English to Farsi, depending on who was speaking at the time. At various points during the trial, French and Spanish were being translated simultaneously into Farsi and English. Headsets provided in the court were an absolute essential for following the proceedings. In the end, the interpreters' fees totalled $298,000. Upgrades to the courtroom and courthouse, including the multilingual interpretation booths, the prisoners' box large enough to hold the three accused, and the new audio-visual system cost $216,000. This was a high-profile case and everything had to be functioning perfectly.

The trial opened the morning of October 20, 2011. Dozens of members of the public and representatives from a dozen or more newspapers, magazines, television, and radio queued up to get into the main courtroom. About half an hour before the scheduled 10 am start, Crown attorney Gerard Laarhuis strode across the upstairs foyer between the courtroom and the Crown's offices. Wished good luck by a bystander, Laarhuis turned and said, "We don't need luck, we need justice."

The long-awaited trial got off to a shaky start. As the 12 jurors walked into the courtroom, one man stood out because of the white Toronto Maple Leafs hockey jersey he was wearing. He stood to address the judge.

"The stress is just killing me," the man said.

"That's good enough for me," replied the judge, dismissing him from duty. The female alternate was then added to the official jury of 12, tipping the balance to seven women and five men. The second alternate was also sent home and Maranger gave the jurors their instructions for the trial.

Then Crown attorney Laurie Lacelle positioned a lectern in front of the jury, laid out the pages with her opening remarks, and launched into a detailed explanation of the case that was succinct and disturbing in its description of what she called "the planned and pre-meditated murders of their family members."

Lacelle outlined the family's history of moving around the world, what Rona's diary would reveal about life in the home, the physical and mental abuse that occurred, the girls' relationships that got them in trouble with their parents, the school reports, and Zainab's sudden departure from the home.

Then she outlined the facts pointing to a conspiracy to

murder: the Google searches, the cellphone records, the late-night encounter at the Kingston East Motel, the police interviews and interrogations, hours of wiretaps, post-mortems on the bodies, the unfolding Kingston Police investigation, and the chilling theory that the car containing the four bodies did not just roll into the canal but was pushed in by someone driving the second family vehicle.

"At the close of the case, after all the evidence has been heard, the Crown will ask you to find Tooba, Shafia, and Hamed guilty of the murders of Rona, Zainab, Sahar, and Geeti," said Lacelle.

Then Laarhuis called the Crown's first witness, Kingston Police forensic identification officer Julia Moore.

Julia Moore was the police photographer of record at Kingston Mills on June 30, 2009. On her photographic tour of the Mills, she came across the three shards of plastic in the grass on the opposite side of the rocky outcrop from the lock itself. Moore photographed a black scuff mark on the side of the curb along Kingston Mills Road. She found another five pieces of plastic at the side of the lock, where the car appeared to have entered the water, and photographed them. There were also the two plastic letters, an S and an E. At the edge of the lock, Moore took pictures of striations that appeared to be freshly cut into the stone wall. The locks along the Rideau Canal were made of hand-carved stone brought from nearby quarries in the late-1820s.

A series of photos was shown of the black Nissan being hoisted out of the water by a crane. Moore had photographed the back end of the car with the S and E missing from the word "Sentra." Moore testified about the control settings in the car: the headlight switch was off, as was the wiper switch; the key was in the ignition but in the off setting; the car was in the lowest gear;

the ceiling light switch was off — and, perhaps oddest of all, the two front seats were reclined far back.

# Reconstruction...

THE physical evidence gathered from the cars was crucial. Constable Chris Prent, a collision reconstruction expert with the Ontario Provincial Police, was brought onto the case in September of 2009 to recreate what happened at the locks the night of June 29-30, and conducted a careful examination of the two Shafia vehicles. With Gananoque Police constable Gordon Boulton, a licensed mechanic, Prent went to see both vehicles at the Kingston Police station.

They took the wheels off the Nissan and found the brakes in good working order. They checked the throttle. Both vehicles were mechanically sound. Prent noted the other irregularities about how the Nissan was found — the headlights off, no one wearing seatbelts, the ignition off, and the car in the lowest gear.

The reclined seats, he said, would have made it "unnatural to be operating this motor vehicle." Prent turned his attention to the vehicles in relation to the physical layout at Kingston Mills. Even though the Nissan was facing back towards the edge it had fallen over, he decided the car had gone in head first. He determined that, from the scrapes on the left side of the Nissan, the car had gotten hung up on the wooden step attached to the lock gate. (This was probably because the car had front-wheel drive, which meant it needed traction to keep moving.) "When it resisted the step, it resisted forward motion and got hung up," Prent said.

There was another snag. As the front axle of the Nissan rolled over the edge of the lock wall, the undercarriage would have dropped down, again stopping the forward motion. "It would require a certain force to be applied to the rear of the vehicle to keep it moving," said Prent. "It's my opinion the Lexus [was] being applied to the left rear of the Nissan ... and [was] being rotated away from the step into the canal."

When they put the Nissan on the hoist, Prent could see where undercoating had been peeled away and there was excessive gouging to the frame, signs of how the car rotated as it went over the edge into the water. As it hit the water, the Nissan began a slow, counter-clockwise rotation until it was facing where it had gone in.

Prent was asked about the additional damage to the Lexus that Hamed had reported to Montreal police in the grocery store lot. It was, he said, a clear attempt to cover up the damage from the locks.

Examining the damage to both cars, and in particular the scrapes along the bottom of the Nissan, Prent was unequivocable in his conclusion: "It's my opinion the Lexus was used to push the Nissan over the edge of the canal into the water."

This contact also explained the damages to the Lexus's headlight and missing letters from the back of the Nissan. Prent was adamant that only by applying force from behind could the Nissan have finished its deadly slide.

Yet there remained a hitch to the Crown and police theory. If the Nissan was being driven while being bumped into the gate step, who was driving?

Gordon Boulton, the cop-mechanic, testified as to how the car operated and how the scenario described by Chris Prent could have been acted out. In fact, Boulton got a 2004 Nissan Sentra just like the Shafias' and did some experimenting of his own. The particular model of Nissan owned by the Shafias was equipped with an automatic stick shift located in the console between the two front seats. To get the car out of park, the ignition must be turned on and taken out of the lock position and the brake pedal must also be pressed down.

If the car was running and put into neutral, Boulton said, the driver could get out of the vehicle and leave it sitting stationary. With the driver's side window rolled down — as it was found on the bottom of the lake — all a person would have to do is reach in and pull the shift stick back to put the car in gear — again, as it was found in the water.

Boulton ran this exact experiment on the test Nissan. "I was surprised," he told the court. "It accelerated rather quickly." If the car were to jump forward and get stuck on the step, it would be possible for the person now outside the car to reach back in and merely shut the car off using the key situated on the steering column, turning out the headlights in the process.

When the car was recovered, police found the key was off and the stick shift was in the lowest gear. This scenario, of course, raised further questions. Were the four women dead or alive, conscious or unconscious, when the car entered the lake and water began to seep inside? Why would anyone who was conscious not have tried to escape from the car? Great expectations were held out for the man who might answer these and other nagging questions — Dr. Christopher Milroy, the forensic pathologist who examined the bodies at the Ottawa General Hospital.

# The autopsies...

GOING into the trial, Kingston Police never said exactly how and when the women died or why they would have passively remained in the car as it filled with water — unless, of course, they were already dead or, at the very least, unconscious. And if they were unconscious, had they been drugged, gassed, strangled, or smothered — or struck over the head?

The post-mortem and toxicology reports did not offer the precise conclusions everyone had been hoping for. "Nothing significant came out of toxicology," said Dr. Milroy. No traces of barbituates, carbon monoxide, cocaine, hydromorphine, oxycontin, or sedatives such as valium were found in the bodies. No alcohol. None of the date rape drug, gama-hydroxibuterate (ghb). No sleeping pills. "There was nothing we could have tested for that really wasn't tested for," concluded Milroy.

Even two bottled drinks and a Thermos bottle of tea found in the Kingston East Motel room tested negative for anything unusual. What Milroy could say for certain was that the four women died by drowning. From the pathologist's point of view, the Shafia case was an easy one to investigate because of the freshness of the bodies. In such situations, the bodies will display expanded lungs that overlap in the middle and frothy fluid in the airway — signs of a "wet drowning" — which is typical of 90% of cases. The women, in other words, were alive when they drowned. Water went into the airways with the result that their bodies were unable to transfer oxygen to their blood supply. The chemical changes in the blood then affected their heart function.

What Milroy couldn't say for certain — and this was crucial — was where the women drowned. "We were not able to determine whether they were alive and drowned [in the car] or had drowned elsewhere and been placed in the car," he said. "I cannot say with any certainty whether they were conscious or unconscious when they were drowned ... They were not incapacitated by drugs. They were not incapacitated by natural disease."

Milroy was asked by Crown attorney Gerard Laarhuis what would have happened if the women had been drowned, taken out of the water, and placed in the car — a suggestion of pre-drowning. A victim might involuntarily cough out the water, the doctor responded, but at some point the damage is irreversible and the heart will stop.

Milroy then noted another common drowning symptom that he found on the bodies — bruising in the necks. As people drown and become unconscious, he said, they may have seizures that cause head and neck movements that result in bruising. "I would call it seizure-related bruising," he concluded.

However, Milroy then described something unusual: bruising on the inside of the scalp on the crown of the heads of three of the four victims — Rona, Zainab, and Geeti. Photos taken by Kingston Police of the scalps cut and peeled back were shown in the courtroom.

The pathologist described what he found on Rona's head. "It's a fairly substantial area of bruising. They could occur in one impact or they could represent two impacts," he said. "It's not the severest of impacts. I would call this a moderate impact." He reckoned it occurred in the hours leading up to Rona's death. "It's a moderate force or firm impact. But neither is it a trivial tap," he said.

Zainab's scalp bruising was described as "less significant" and could have been produced by minor bumps on the head. Geeti's bruising was the result of "one impact to the head." Bruising can only take place, said Milroy, when a person is alive and the heart is beating.

"All the bruising is fresh. They could have occurred in the period just before death." Of significance to Milroy was the fact that the bruises were found in similar areas on the heads of three victims. "It clearly requires explanation," he said. "There is a relative absence of injury elsewhere on the bodies."

He was asked if the bruises could have been caused by their heads hitting the ceiling of the car as it plunged into the water. "It would have to be a relatively firm surface for that to occur," he replied.

In his cross-examination of the doctor, defence lawyer Peter Kemp created a hypothetical scene of panic in the car as it tumbled into the lake and began to fill with water. He suggested the women, alive and fully conscious, would try to move upward where a pocket of air remained near the car's ceiling.

"They might strive to get out of the car," Milroy agreed. "They could even flail out. Clash heads. These are all possibilities." Kemp suggested they could have hit the rear window. "Possibility," said Milroy.

Kemp asked the doctor how long it would take someone to drown if their head was held under water. "It's probably gonna take two or three minutes," said Milroy, "about ten minutes for the heart to stop."

Kemp wanted to know the likelihood of someone's being able to hit three different people over the head with just enough force to render all of them unconscious, yet not kill them. Milroy said that would be hard to say. "It would be unpredictable when they would lose consciousness," he answered.

Lawyer Patrick McCann would also pursue this line of questioning. "I think it's unlikely," Milroy told him, "[that] you could deliver three blows and render them unconscious with just three blows." Milroy acknowledged that he had not found the bruising suspicious at the time of examination.

"There was no evidence they'd been subject to an attack or subject to a restraint by other parties," he said. "I certainly released the bodies that day."

In his re-examination, Laarhuis reinforced the Crown position as to the similarity of the bruising to three of the victims. "What the jury has to consider is a scenario in which," said Laarhuis, "alive and in the dark, why you only get bruises in one area."

# Mojab...

THE Crown called its final witness on December 5, 2011, Professor Shahrzad Mojab, an academic from the University of Toronto, specializing in Middle Eastern honour killings. Since Justice Maranger had declared Mojab qualified as an expert witness, the Crown had to be careful not to lead Mojab with questions that would result in her speaking specifically about the Shafia case, but to allow her to speak in general terms about honour killings.

In her testimony, Mojab described a woman's body as "the repository of family honour" in some Middle Eastern cultures — that family status depends on the control of female sexuality., She testified that, in such cultures, things like a woman's refusing to enter an arranged marriage, or being implicated in an alleged adultery, or being the victim of a sexual assault, "can trigger an attack upon her life." Mojab was also quick to point out that honour killings are not particular to Islam — that Hindus, Jews, and Christians around the world may also practise forms of it. The notion of honour as something that must be protected, she said, "predates religion."

"The honour," she continued, "belongs to the patrilineal, the male gender of the family. That's where it belongs and that's why the act of killing is acted and perpetrated by male members of the family." Yet, she said, "there are cases [where] female members of the family and, in particular mothers, participate."

While speaking in general terms, Mojab's testimony clearly supported the Crown's theory about how and why the four women might have been killed.

"The patriarch is known," she said. "It's clear who is in power in the family ... through the control of the woman's body and sexuality and women's behaviour."

The jury had already heard the wiretaps with Mohammad Shafia ranting about how his daughters had shamed him, offended his honour with their photos of themselves and their boyfriends. They'd also heard Tooba carefully defending one of her surviving daughters and one of her sons to Mohammad, telling him they were good children.

"Mothers are often in the middle," testified Mojab, "because they have to negotiate the powers of the male members of the family."

This would also become an important point of law that Justice Maranger would cover with the jury when he sent them out to deliberate. Even if one of the accused didn't directly participate in the act of murder, they could be found guilty of first-degree murder by assisting in the killing, by giving tools, acting as a lookout or, without even being present when the killing took place, by making it easier for the murder to be committed.

Mojab went further in her testimony, pointing out that the female body itself represents the structure of the family. If the woman or girl is promiscuous, "it means they are not obeying the order. They are not submitting to the power of the patriarch of the family." Compliance, she said, covered everything from appearance, to choosing a partner, to "submitting to the power of the patriarch of the family." Control is exerted in the control of social relations, divorce requests, and forced marriages. For young women, particularly in Western cultures, said Mojab, "it's a very difficult task to negotiate and navigate" all of these controls and demands.

Mojab pointed out that even fathers who kill for honour love their daughters. Family honour is also "for the sake of children, for also giving them honour. It is part of the continuum of love and care." With this kind of thinking, she said, killing becomes an "expected act. It is expected the honour of the family [will] be restored and controlled."

Experts have also documented that the planning of honour killings may take place over several years. It begins, said Mojab, with disappointment, moving into physical violence, psychological pressure, financial restrictions, leading to "the gradual escalation of violence and then the moment of killing."

Then, reminiscent of Mohammad's rantings on the wiretaps, Mojab described how the women are ultimately blamed for their own deaths. If the woman had only listened, said Mojab, "she would have saved her life. These are the arguments we hear all the time, that it was only a matter of dressing differently. Small matters like that cause the death of the woman."

The members of the jury would have to ask themselves what any citizen of Canada would ask: "But does this justify the murders of four women, three of them the young daughters of their killer? Can anything justify that?"

# In his own defence...

**A**S the trial moved into its second full month, defence lawyer
Peter Kemp rose on the morning of December 8 and called
his client to testify. Mohammad Shafia stood up in the prisoners'
box and calmly made his way to the witness stand. He tested the
interpreters' headset and then swore an oath on the Koran to tell the
truth before Justice Robert Maranger and the jury.

This was a significant development, considering that on
November 3, the court learned that Shafia had been taken to
hospital the previous night with an unspecified "serious" medical
condition. At that point, the trial went into limbo until November
8 when Shafia returned to his regular seat in the prisoners' docket,
wearing his usual checked sport jacket and looking none the worse
for wear.

Now, a month later, he was relaxed and clearly prepared to
talk. Under questioning by Kemp, through the usual series of interpretations, Shafia related his early life in Kabul, his rise to success as
an electronics businessman, and the family's many moves to escape
persecution and find a better life. He talked about how he met both
his wives, Rona and Tooba, and came to marry them.

Kemp's strategy soon became clear. He was asking Shafia the
difficult questions up front, or at least working around the fringes of
the more damning evidence heard and seen so far.

Was he a devout Muslim? "I am a Muslim, normal, like other Muslims," he answered.

The Koran prevents Muslims from murdering or killing anyone? Yes.

Births and deaths are predetermined by God? "It is God who determines the date of someone's death," said Shafia. "No one else."

Kemp asked him about the importance of religion in marriage. "Mr. Kemp," he replied, "this depends on the girl. If she wants someone to be out of my religion, I will ask my daughter and tell her this is not good. If she insists on this, this is not good — but this is her life."

Shafia also insisted he never had any issues with any of his daughters' clothing or makeup. The father and daughter clashed over Ammar, her Pakistani boyfriend. He said he approached Zainab, advising her to continue with her education instead of marrying him. Zainab told him she would consider it.

"I did what a father will do," he testified.

After the marriage broke down, Shafia said Zainab called him in Dubai. "We had greetings and she said, Daddy, I want to offer my apologies to you that I didn't listen to what you told me," he recounted. "I said, I have already forgiven you.'"

Shafia began crying on the witness stand, recalling how Zainab came to his room after he returned from Dubai to apologize to him once more. "I gave her a hundred dollars and I kissed her face. I didn't say anything else to her," he said.

Shafia also insisted that there was never any plan to leave Rona in Europe after the family came to Canada. "My conscience and our conscience never allowed this."

Why, then, did he lie and tell immigration authorities she was a cousin? "Because the lawyer told me, and I knew that [also], two wives will not be accepted."

He insisted Rona was always welcome to eat at the table with the family and that she did so. "I never hit Rona but I swore at her," he said.

Then he talked about the photographs of Zainab and Sahar that provoked him to swear and curse them on the police wiretaps.

Shafia claimed he never saw the provocative pictures of his daughters until around the time of their funerals when his sons were cleaning the bedrooms for guests to stay. Only then did he learn about Sahar's boyfriend Ricardo.

"I was not happy with seeing this picture. I didn't think of my children this way. I never expected my children [would do] this thing. My children did a lot of cruelty toward me," he said. "I'm not sure if the mom knew about this. They hid this from me. I swore because I did not expect this thing from my children."

Shafia was asked to explain why he would exhort the devil to shit on the graves of his dead daughters. "Yes, I heard it in the court," he replied. "To me it means the devil will go out and check their graves." When he called the girls filthy, he said, "I was actually cursing myself. I was swearing at myself."

Then Shafia offered interesting takes on the conversations he had with Fazil Javid and Latif Hyderi. He said he never tried to engage Fazil in a plot to kill Zainab because "the minute he said it was Fazil, I hung up on him. Not even two seconds. I turned if off."

He was suspicious of the uncle's call. "Latif was the one who cancelled this marriage [to Ammar Wahid] and basically forced my daughter to withdraw," he charged.

Kemp reminded Shafia that he sounded "quite angry" in the

wiretaps. He admitted that he was upset because "Zainab, she didn't accept my words, and Sahar, because I saw those pictures."

Shafia then insisted that both cars and all 10 people went to the Kingston East Motel the night of the deaths and that Zainab came and asked Tooba for the keys to the Nissan.

"She gave the key. Rona was behind her," he said.

Most importantly, perhaps, he said he never realized where the four had died until he and Tooba and Hamed went there with police on July 18, 2009. "I didn't know this area Kingston Mills by its name."

It was also during this day of examination that Shafia insisted he was travelling alone to Montreal on July 27 when, nearing Kingston, he got a phone call to return to Niagara Falls.

When it was her turn to question him, Crown attorney Laurie Lacelle wanted Shafia to explain his treatment of Rona, suggesting his first wife had become Tooba's servant.

"I beg you, dear respected lady," said Shafia, "she was a member of my family. In all my life I spent more money for her than for Tooba." Shafia insisted Rona was referred to as his cousin only for immigration purposes. He said the children had never been told to hide the true relationship. "The children knew her as their aunt," he said.

As for the wiretaps, Lacelle highlighted the difference between how Shafia spoke of his daughters and how he talked to Hamed when, as the two of them sat in a police cruiser under arrest, Shafia said to his son: "I commend you to God."

"You never said that to your daughters, did you?" Lacelle pointed out. "You said, may the devil shit on their graves."

Shafia said he found the photos of the girls in underwear and with boyfriends upsetting. "I was not happy with this. They hid this from me," he said. "The pictures when she was in the laps of boys. I saw these pictures. They were bad pictures."

Again, echoing the expert testimony of Shahrzad Mojab, Shafia placed the blame for Zainab's troubles squarely on his daughter's actions. "She destroyed her life because she didn't listen to our advice," he said matter-of-factly.

Lacelle's cross-examination went into a second day. She grilled Shafia about the trip to Niagara Falls and why Hamed's cellphone was recorded being used off the Westbrook Road tower west of Kingston right in the middle of the vacation. Hamed was never without his cellphone, so police believed he participated in a scouting mission that took the pair to Kingston Mills.

"On the 27th it was me alone," Shafia now acknowledged. During interrogation, Shafia had been silent on the matter. "Hamed was not with me," he stated.

Lacelle wanted to know why the family started out so late from Niagara Falls on June 29 to return to Montreal. Checkout from the first room was 11:06 am but they didn't leave the second room until 6:46 pm, "even though everyone was ready to go. You decided to start a seven- or eight-hour trip at night?"

"That was the decision everyone made," Shafia responded.

"I suggest you started that trip late at night because you wanted those kids to be asleep when you got to Kingston," Lacelle countered.

"When you are tired you can go to sleep," Shafia said. "[It] wasn't the intention for the children to go to sleep."

Lacelle moved on to the scene in Kingston, Shafia insisting that when he and Hamed went to find a motel that Tooba was sitting with the car just a short distance up Highway 15.

Lacelle accused Mohammad, Tooba, and Hamed of killing the women.

"We never gave permission to ourselves," he said. "All of our children came to the hotel. We never allowed ourselves to do this ... The mom would be the first to complain. How is it possible someone would do that to their children?"

"You might do that if you thought they were whores," Lacelle said.

He only considered Zainab and Sahar to be that way, Shafia answered, after seeing the suggestive photographs after their deaths. "The two others, they were innocent and one was just a child."

Shafia also dismissed the wiretaps, even what sounded like concern for the possibility that cameras might have recorded their actions at Kingston Mills. "I wish there was a camera," he told Lacelle. "We have no worry about the camera. Whatever evidence could be found about my children I would be happy about that ... I wish there was a camera so we would not be in this trouble."

When Shafia was recorded saying the girls "messed up," he said it was directed at Zainab's taking the car for a joyride. "This is a bad thing she did," he said, "take the car key without permission."

Despite Shafia, Tooba, and Hamed's having told police on several occasions that Zainab was prone to taking the car keys and driving the Nissan, Shafia had this to say: "If we knew they will do such a thing and take the key and drive, if I knew that, I would have prevented that action." Yet Tooba allegedly turned over the keys to her untrustworthy daughter without hesitation.

Lacelle had a theory why Shafia was vehement that he would repeat his actions even if they hoisted him onto the gallows. "You chose to kill them," she said.

Shafia replied that murdering his daughters and first wife would not do anything to restore honour. "For me, anyone who kills a child or daughter, that person really becomes shameless," Shafia reasoned. "I don't call that honour."

The defence lawyers finished their re-examinations of Shafia around noon on Friday, December 9. They told the court that on Monday they would call two of the surviving Shafia children to testify. As it turned out, only one of them, the son, would be called to the stand.

# A son testifies...

HIS appearance that morning had a dramatic effect on Shafia and Tooba. Now 18, he was just 15 the night of July 21, 2009, when police arrived at the rue Bonnivet home to take him and his two sisters into protective custody. He was a young man now, waving shyly to his parents as he took his seat in the witness stand. When he was sworn into court, the sound of his voice caused his parents to cry.

Before examination by Peter Kemp began, court watched a long interview from the night of July 21, at a Montreal police station, between the 15-year-old and Kingston Police detective Sean Bambrick, a specialist in the child physical and sex abuse unit. On the tape, Bambrick questions the boy about all the tumult in the house prior to the Niagara Falls vacation.

Then Bambrick gets him to recount events from the night of June 29-30. He is vague about what took place that night because he was sleeping in the Lexus, but did remember it was precisely 1:53 am when his father woke him up to go into the motel. Then he gave more details.

"He gave me the keys and he was, like, in 18, he told me 18, so I just entered 18 with my sister ... and my little sister ... and, yeah, we entered the room and we fell asleep."

He vaguely remembers someone coming to him while he was in bed, maybe a sister or his mother, and asking for his cellphone.

The phone was no longer operating as a phone but the children used it to listen to music. The next morning, they heard their parents talking about family members being missing. He assumed it was Zainab because she had run away before.

As the interview continues, the boy tells Bambrick he can't believe his parents and brother would kill his sisters and Rona. Bambrick asks him if he can recall anyone leaving Niagara Falls while the family was staying there. The boy says that, yes, Hamed and his father went to Toronto to open a bank account related to Shafia's car import business in Dubai.

The boy also talks about the family's trip to Niagara Falls the previous year, in 2008, when they were pulled over at Napanee by Ontario Provincial Police for having all 10 family members in the Lexus. The vehicle was impounded. While Hamed and Shafia took a train back to Montreal to get the van, the rest of the family stayed in a hotel in Kingston. This established for police that the Shafias, even going back a year, had some familiarity with Kingston.

The boy tells the officer that if he thought his parents were involved in a murder conspiracy, he would be the first to turn them in. He portrays himself as the one who stood up to his father when there were family arguments and that he would absorb the physical abuse, particularly during one incident when the children came home late from the mall one night.

"You know, like, I would do the most arguing," he tells Bambrick. "The first time, I was the one who called the cops, you know."

As the video played in the courtroom, the young man began taking notes, preparing for his testimony. It began with questioning by Kemp who addressed the issue of violence in the Shafia home. The young man said that even though his father hit them, it was because he was worried for their safety and that, by the end of these confrontations, they all "understood why he got mad."

On the matter of Zainab's disappearance on April 17, 2009, he completely changed his story from a previous police interview. He had admitted in the video interview that he was the one who called police because the children feared their father's reaction and felt they weren't safe. Now, in court, the young man said none of that was true, suggesting that even the investigating police officers thought they were "joking" with them.

He also downplayed the investigations by child protection workers at the school in both 2008 and 2009. "The teachers felt we were victims and we were abused at home," he told the court. He now said it was a game they played to win sympathy at school and get out of having to do school work. In fact, he said, there was no tension at 8644 rue Bonnivet.

"Sahar was very happy at home," he testified. "It was a very happy, joyful [family], enjoying life. It was just some of the stories we told the teachers for special treatment." The young man said he only learned of Sahar's boyfriend "after her death," despite testimony by Ricardo Sanchez stating they had met.

"The last time I saw the guy — what's his name — I saw him on the news," he testified. "I never saw him before."

He said that Zainab would receive drunken calls from Ammar Wahid, ordering her "to get money from the rest of us."

The young man became the go-between for Zainab and her mother when Zainab was in the shelter. "She was having second thoughts," he testified. "She told me she regretted leaving home and it wasn't the way she thought it would be ... She thought there would be room service."

And he accused his great-uncle, Latif Hyderi, of bullying Zainab into marrying his son, Hussain, on the day her marriage to Wahid was dissolved. "Latif told her, didn't ask her, you're going to marry my son now. Zainab was crying," he recalled. By the time they returned home that day, Latif "was making arrangements and setting dates already."

His recollections now were much clearer about what happened after they checked into the Kingston East Motel. "I wasn't actually asleep. I was lying down," he said. "After a few minutes, I remember Zainab coming in and asking for my cellphone."

Kemp pointed out that, in the video interview, he hadn't been so certain. "When I think about it, I can clearly say it was Zainab," he said.

The young man also said Zainab was eager to drive and that he once had to convince her, when the two of them were driving around the motel parking lot in Niagara Falls, not to take the Nissan out onto the street. "Zainab really wanted to get her driver's licence," he said.

The young man also took responsibility for one of the Google searches on the laptop computer, the one titled, "where to commit murder."

"When I was suicidal, I was trying to find ways and I would search stuff on the Internet like that. I wasn't familiar with the term suicide. I thought murder was the same thing," he said.

In Islam, suicide is strictly forbidden as it is an affront to God, who is the only one who can determine life and death. Yet in the pre-trial interviews, and at the trial, the subject of suicide comes up often in relation to the Shafia children. Statistics tell us that suicide is the third leading cause of death among 15-to-24-year-olds, and the sixth leading cause of death among 5-to-14-year-olds. Teenagers often experience overwhelming feelings of stress, confusion, and self-doubt, along with other fears while growing up. For some teens, suicide may appear to be a solution to their problems. For the Shafia children, stress levels were often very high, as evidenced by their fear of their father and their many pleas for help to teachers and outside agencies.

On the next morning of the trial, Crown attorney Gerard Laarhuis accused the young man of fabricating the story about being at the motel room.

"Zainab never came to the room asking for a phone," said the attorney. "I am just putting it to you. Do you agree?"

"No, I don't," he answered.

Laarhuis said it was actually his mother asking for the phone so they could call Hamed who was on his way to Montreal in the middle of the night. "The story was supposed to be [that] Zainab came and asked for the keys. You got mixed up. You said she came and asked for a cellphone."

Laarhuis then presented evidence from a police wiretap from the night of July 21, when the young man, just taken out of the home along with his sisters, called Hamed. Laarhuis said it was clear from their conversation that he was trying to assure Hamed that he'd given no information to police.

"You didn't want to help the police find the truth did you?" Hamed asked him.

"I told him [Hamed] everything I knew," he replied. "I'm telling him to say what happened. Tell the police what happened."

It's also clear that by the time of this recorded conversation with Hamed, the young man knows and understands the word "suicide." He is pleading with his brother not to make matters worse.

"Don't do anything stupid. 'Cause, Hamed, [if] you guys think of suicide and all that, don't do it, okay?" he tells him. "Look, Hamed, you are 100% caught," he continues.

Hamed warns him to be careful about what he says because the phone may be bugged. In court, Laarhuis accused the young man of already knowing at that point how his sisters and Rona died and who did it.

"The only issue in your mind during this phone conversation was whether police had enough proof," said Laarhuis.

"Enough false proof, yes," he countered.

When the call ends at 3:04 in the morning, Shafia asks Hamed what the police were saying to the younger children and how they responded.

"They said, police from Kingston came and said [they have] 100% proof that the Lexus vehicle hit [the Nissan] from the back," Hamed tells his father. "They [said], for example, uh, we know what happened, why it happened. They asked him lots of things. He said we said the same things."

"[What] they saw in the hotel?" Shafia asks.

"Yeah," says Hamed.

Laarhuis would return to the young man's suicidal feelings, which seemed to heighten around the April 17 when Zainab left the home for the shelter. Yet he couldn't recall the incident in which Sahar had taken pills herself and reported her feelings to school officials and youth protection workers.

"Sahar wasn't suicidal," he said, chalking it up to one of the pranks they played on their teachers. He said the intent of his Google search for "where to commit a murder" was really meant to be how to murder yourself.

"This wasn't some random group of words," Laarhuis suggested.

Even after admitting he read Rona's diary, describing how bitter her life was, the young man described her as being happy and having "many friends."

"Where do you draw the line," Laarhuis asked him, "on manipulating people and telling lies?"

"When it goes too far, I guess," was his answer.

Laarhuis pointed out to the young man that in his testimony he made significant changes to the stories he told police three years earlier. "Where your memory has improved, it's all to the benefit of your mom and dad and Hamed," said the lawyer. "Where your memory hasn't improved are [the] things that aren't helpful to your parents."

# The trial continues...

A S the trial broke for Christmas on December 14, it was unclear whether Tooba and Hamed would be called to testify in the New Year. The non-communication order preventing the Shafias from talking to their children in Montreal was vacated after being in place for three years. Then lawyer Patrick McCann told the court that his client Hamed Shafia would take the stand.

When the trial resumed on January 9, 2012, it wasn't Hamed but his mother, Tooba, who made her way to the witness stand. Tooba's lawyer, David Crowe, led her through her early life. Born in Kabul, Tooba said she came from a family of 16 children. Her father, a pharmacist who owned three drug stores in the city, had 10 sons and six daughters with two wives. Her father's first wife died of breast cancer and Tooba's mother was a divorcée. Most of her siblings were university-educated with professional jobs. Tooba only got to Grade 7 because life was interrupted by the war in Afghanistan. She was home-schooled before being married to Shafia in 1988.

Tooba confirmed that before their family left Dubai for Canada in 2007, there had been an agreement reached with the children. "We decided that until the child graduated, they are not allowed to have a girlfriend or boyfriend or get married," she told the court. There was no physical punishment in the home except the single time Shafia slapped the children when they came home late.

"Shafie had one custom — he used to talk. He used to talk a lot," she said. "If it was a small thing, he made it a big thing." Tooba said the children were tired of his incessant nagging about small issues so they kept information from their father.

Crowe raised the issue of Rona's being restricted in her telephone use in the home and having to make calls from a pay phone in the park. Tooba said it was directly related to one incident in which Rona made a call that lasted 75 minutes while the school was unsuccessfully trying to contact the home.

"I told her very nicely and she said, yes, it was the wrong thing to do," Tooba recalled. She knew nothing about what was in Rona's memoir, having only seen it when the family cleaned up the house and put it in a closet where it was later found by police.

Tooba had a different take on the incident in which Sahar attempted suicide. Her daughter didn't ingest pills, she said, but a preservative used to keep flowers fresh. She also thought her daughter was prone to exaggeration.

"Sahar had a habit," said Tooba. "If she was missing a movie she wanted to see, she would say, I'll kill myself." Tooba said Rona returned from a walk that day to discover Sahar, her adopted child, in distress. "Rona yelled at me," she recalled. "She swore at me. This is what I remember." It was on one such occasion that Rona recorded in her diary that Tooba said, "She can go to hell. Let her kill herself." Tooba denied she ever called Rona her "servant."

In her two interviews with police, Tooba told different versions of what happened on the night of June 29-30. In the first, she had stayed with the four women in the Nissan while Hamed and Shafia went to find a motel. In the second, she told RCMP inspector Shahin Mehdizadeh that she waited with them at the locks and, when they returned, she and Hamed were together when they heard the Nissan splash into the water.

On the witness stand, she had a new story to tell. She was now saying that they never went to the locks that night but specifically waited in the car along Highway 15 while the men went just down the road to the Kingston East Motel.

"I was very tired. I reclined the seat and I lay down. I don't know how long it took them," she said.

The men returned in the Lexus and she followed them to the motel. This differs from Hamed's and Shafia's versions. They said by the time they were pulling out of the motel lot to go back to the Nissan, Tooba was already driving in their direction. The motel manager said he stayed up for at least a half-hour watching for the Lexus to return. It didn't. He never saw the Nissan at all.

Tooba still insisted that everyone, including Rona and her daughters who died, got to the motel that night. She and Shafia and their three surviving children were in their room when "there was a knock at the door. Zainab came and said, 'Mother, can you give me the keys to the car because there's clothing in the trunk [and] I want to get it.'" Tooba changed for bed and went to sleep.

"I don't know anything until the next morning," she told the court.

Tooba's explanation for the story she told Mehdizadeh about hearing the car go into the water was that she was only trying to protect Hamed. She claimed to have gotten only "three hours totally" of sleep from the time of the deaths on June 30 to the day of their arrests on July 21. Specifically, she wanted to protect Hamed from torture. She claimed that when they were arrested, a Persian-speaking female police officer from Toronto told her that Hamed would be tortured with cold water. Tooba said it evoked recollections of torture performed in Afghanistan.

"I didn't want to send Hamed to torture," she said. "I put myself in that spot to show Hamed was innocent ... None of that was true. I said this to show I was there to get Hamed out of that position. I didn't know what else to say."

Again, police had placed a wiretap in the police cruiser and recorded the conversation between Tooba and the police officer. What the officer actually told her was that Hamed was arrested and would be cooling his heels and drinking cold water in jail. There was no mention of torture.

Gerard Laarhuis's cross-examination of Tooba began with trying to establish when she might be telling the truth or not, even on the witness stand. Tooba said the only time she lied was during her interrogation, to protect her son. Laarhuis pointed out that she had not been forthcoming at any time about the fact that Rona was Shafia's first wife.

"I didn't see it was necessary to say that to the police," she said. "He was not an immigration lawyer." In other words, she would lie to a police officer but not to an immigration official.

"You said she was a cousin and not Shafie's wife. That was a lie and you knew it," Laarhuis pressed her. ("Shafie" was the named used by both Tooba and Rona to address Mohammad.)

"I had a lot of pain in front of me. I lost my three daughters," she replied.

"Does stress turn you into a liar?" Laarhuis asked.

"In that condition, sir, that wasn't a lie. We told the Canadian government she was a cousin," she said. "Indeed, sometimes when a person is under stress, that person will tell lies."

"Do you feel under pressure now?"

"That pressure, no," said Tooba.

When police searched the house on July 21, they found the black suitcase containing a number of photos of Sahar, Zainab, and Rona inside. It was the Crown's assertion that Hamed planned to take those pictures, downloaded from the girls' phones, to Dubai to show his father that the girls had been deceptive — and that they incited Shafia to kill his daughters and then to make the angry statements captured on wiretaps.

Tooba said she had found Sahar's pink Disney album with the photos of Sahar and Zainab and took them out and hid them in the suitcase sometime around July 4, 5, or 6, just prior to the funerals. This would imply that the photos were not available to provoke Shafia to plan the murders. On July 2, however, the Shafias allowed a CTV news crew into their home to talk about their loss. In the video, Shafia is crying and showing the reporter the pink photo album with pictures of his daughters.

Laarhuis suggested that if her husband had been looking at the album containing the inflammatory pictures of his daughters, "Shafie would be ballistic."

Tooba said there was more than one album of that type in the house. "I can tell you that I have one or two. Maybe one or two," she said.

"Do you have one or two?" Laarhuis continued.

"Two or one," Tooba replied. "We have many albums."

"You're seen flipping through this photo album. It was this one, wasn't it?" Laarhuis asked.

"The one we showed to the media was another one. The one with the naked pictures I didn't show to the media," Tooba insisted.

174

Frustrated by her answers, Laarhuis arranged to show the actual CTV interview in court. "It's clearly the princess book ... we have in the courtroom today," he said after the viewing.

"Yes, that's correct," Tooba admitted, adding that perhaps Shafia didn't flip to the back of the album where the photos were located.

Tooba denied receiving a call from her brother Fazil, warning her that Shafia was plotting to murder Zainab. She also said she had never heard of the concept of honour killing in Afghanistan.

She added new information about the Niagara Falls trip: that Shafia had left them twice, once to go to Toronto with Hamed to open a bank account, and a second time to go to Montreal for business. "I remember the children asking, where is your father?" Tooba testified. "He told me once he was going to Montreal."

She acknowledged that she was upset at Hamed for not telling them about having followed the women to Kingston Mills that night and watching them drown. "If it was accidental, he should have told us," she said.

The wiretaps were more difficult for Tooba to explain. Why did they return to the van after being shown around the locks on July 18 and talk about being there several times before — but not tell police about that? Why didn't she tell the RCMP's Mehdizadeh they had stopped there for a bathroom break on June 24 on the way to Niagara Falls? The officer had shown her an aerial photo of Kingston Mills. "I didn't know the name of the place to specifically tell him," she said.

Laarhuis was relentless in his questioning. Plan A of their murder plot, he said to Tooba, was to tell police that Zainab took the keys. When Mehdizadeh pressured her, she went to Plan B, which was to implicate Shafia but not herself and Hamed. When Mehdi-zadeh established that Hamed was the lone driver of the Lexus that night, and it was used to push the Nissan into the water, Tooba had to resort to Plan C, saying she couldn't remember and then, eventually, that she had lied to save Hamed from torture.

# Defence

# summations...

THE jury began to hear the defence lawyers' summations on January 24, 2012. Hamed Shafia never took the stand. Instead, the jury was left to consider his role in the deaths based on the statements he had made to Moosa Hadi — essentially, that he had left his sisters and Rona to drown inside the Nissan; that he did not call police; and that he stole off into the night to Montreal where he staged an accident to cover up damage to the Lexus that had, according to him, been an accident in the first place.

Peter Kemp was first up in front of the jury, describing his client, Mohammad Shafia, as a man who directed all of his life's efforts and energies to his family. When his first wife couldn't bear him children, he found a woman who could — that is how much he wanted to have a family.

Despite all the allegations of physical abuse in the family, said Kemp, none of the photographs entered as evidence during the trial showed any marks on the four dead women. He portrayed Rona's sister Diba as "one of the worst witnesses I've ever heard." He wondered why Fahima Vorgetts never called police when Rona was making so many awful disclosures of abuse to her over the phone.

Kemp said it was Latif Hyderi who broke up the marriage between Zainab and Ammar Wahid and that he was lying about Shafia's statement that he wanted to kill his daughter Zainab. The lawyer characterized the murder plot described by Rona's brother Fazil Javid as "totally unbelievable."

As for the wiretap evidence, Kemp reminded the jury that it was a habit of Shafia's to swear and that he did so to calm himself. It was only the hurt caused by his daughters' actions that made him talk that way. "Mohammad Shafia took his duties as a father very seriously. He insisted on giving his daughters the best advice he could and let them decide," said Kemp.

Kemp's response to the Crown's murder theory was that there was no time for the four separate killings to occur. "It was an accident that could happen very quickly. For a murder, it's a totally different time frame," he said. He addressed the Crown's insinuation that the four women may have been pre-drowned by arguing that four people would not sit calmly inside the Nissan while the others disappeared one by one. Even then, how could the bodies be placed back in the car without being seen in such a public place? "The problem would have been almost insurmountable," said Kemp.

He explained the bruising on the victims' heads as resulting from the car's plunge into the water. "Water is gushing in through the window. You would immediately become disoriented," said Kemp. "They would have been climbing all over each other trying to get out of the car. They would have been unsuccessful."

Kemp referred to Hamed's account of that night as told to Moosa Hadi. Until that confession became public, Shafia had no idea what had really happened to his daughters and first wife. "He didn't know about the fake accident in Montreal and he didn't know about any damage to the Lexus," said Kemp.

Tooba's lawyer, David Crowe, also challenged the Crown's murder theory in some detail. If the four women had been pre-drowned in the basin at Kingston Mills, they would have had to agree to go into that area in the first place. "You could not do that in the bathrooms because those bathrooms are locked up," he said, with only boaters being provided keys at night.

Crowe described Mehdizadeh's interrogation of Tooba as "unrelenting" and that he "had her cornered for several hours," calling her a liar at least "500 times." Even when she fabricates a story, he said, "at no point does she acknowledge she was involved in the deaths of the deceased." Besides, she recanted everything the next day.

Even though Tooba had come across Rona's diary after her death, Crowe pointed out that she didn't throw it away. "Certainly they [the entries] weren't complimentary to her and showed relations between her and Rona at times weren't good," he said. "It wasn't hidden. It was there for police to find."

Hamed's lawyer Patrick McCann led off his summation by also challenging the speculative nature of the murder theory. The women would not have submitted to such a scenario, he said, therefore they had to have been incapacitated. However, there was no bruising on their bodies to suggest a struggle, no wet clothes found among the accused and no drugs in the victims' bodies. "The whole thing simply defies logic," he said.

McCann suggested that the women displayed contradictory

behaviours. Zainab claimed to have loved Ammar Wahid yet made a 911 call to police on June 2, saying that he was threatening her. "What can we say about Zainab? ... I don't want to criticize someone who's deceased," he said. "Maybe she's a bit spoiled. Maybe she's used to getting her way. Unfortunately, we don't know because we haven't seen her."

McCann suggested that Sahar was equally erratic in her behaviour, which he attributed largely to the fact that she was dating her first boyfriend. "Geeti was a bit of rebel and didn't care much," he said. "Is that a motive to murder Geeti? You just have to shake your head and wonder." "Boy crazy" teenagers "pushing the envelope" is how he summed up their actions.

McCann decided to tackle Hamed's interview with Moosa Hadi head-on by presenting it as the final version of what happened the night the women died. "He ran to the edge. Called their names. Ran back to the Lexus and grabbed a rope out of the Lexus. We've seen that rope," McCann began.

"He dropped the rope in. Called their names. Honked the horn a couple of times. Nothing ... Then he made a terrible, terrible decision, thinking: No one knows I came here.' And he's 18 at the time. He's a kid. If I go to Montreal, no one will know the difference.'"

Hamed sat in the prisoners' box staring straight ahead as his lawyer continued. McCann told the jurors that the only reason the deaths attracted such wide attention was because of how the story was labelled. "This is not a big story if it's not an honour killing," he said. "It's an accident."

The lawyer asked the jury to focus on what was known for certain about the case, not on the circumstantial evidence. "We know that the Crown theory cannot work unless Rona and the girls were incapacitated by drowning beforehand. That is impossible. The evidence just doesn't stand up," he said.

"Hamed is guilty of being stupid — morally blameworthy. Other than that, he is not responsible for the girls' deaths, nor were his parents. It's time to put an end to this Kafka-esque two years."

# Crown summation...

IN her summation, Crown attorney Laurie Lacelle chose to re-focus the trial on the victims. Rona, Zainab, Sahar, and Geeti, she said, had one thing in common: they all desired their freedom. They wanted to go out with friends, to have boyfriends, to wear the clothes they liked, to be free of surveillance, and to escape the physical and mental abuse in the Shafia home.

Their lives, however, were in the hands of the people who should have been their protectors — Shafia, Tooba, and Hamed. "No one else had the exclusive opportunity to kill them," said Lacelle. "And no one else thought they should die."

For the next two hours, Lacelle would repeat the Crown's case. She stopped partway through her summation, at around 4 pm, planning to finish the next day.

At about 9:15 the next morning, with the usual throng of Kingston trial watchers and growing media contingent waiting for the courtroom doors to open, Kingston Police detective Chris Scott appeared on the landing of the courthouse stairway and calmly asked everyone to leave the building. Someone had phoned in a bomb threat to police that morning. The entire courthouse was evacuated as a heavy contingent of specialized tactical squad police and sniffer dogs arrived. The jury was sent away but asked to remain on standby. The three accused were quickly ushered into a waiting van and taken away from the site.

As enthralling as the testimony had been at times, this interruption gave the satellite TV news trucks something new to report on. The Kingston Mills murder trial had spilled into the streets of the city. It wasn't until 1:30 that news reporters began to hear that they might soon be admitted back into the building. When they were, the entire scene inside the courthouse had radically changed. Where before maybe one or two police officers and scattered security personnel had represented the sum total of security, the foyer was now crawling with cops in full swat gear. The dormant metal detector that sat gathering dust outside the courtroom was brought down to the main front door and shocked into life. One at a time, reporters and members of the public had to give their names, present photo identification, submit to baggage checks, and clear the detector. It had all gone so smoothly, so low-key and Kingston-like, until now, in the waning days of the trial.

Just after 2 pm, the three accused were brought back into the courtroom. Justice Maranger arrived shortly after, while members of the public continued to filter in. The jury returned and settled back into the job at hand. "I tell you, expect the unexpected," the judge told them.

Lacelle launched back into her summation as two alert young tactical squad cops sat at attention at either front corner of the courtroom. However, in order to reduce the distraction caused by people coming in, Maranger recessed again until 2:45 pm.

When the trial re-started for the second time, Lacelle wasted no time getting back to the heart of the Crown case. She said the four women who died were considered by Shafia, Tooba, and Hamed to be "the diseased limb on the family tree. Their solution was to remove the diseased limb in its entirety and trim the tree back to the good wood."

She reminded the jury of the serious plotting going on behind the scenes: Hamed's Google searches about "where to commit a murder" and "can a prisoner control his real estate"; his trip to Grand-Remous on June 20 to search for a suitable murder site; the purchase of the 2004 Nissan — a "relatively cheap car" — that could be more easily submerged than the family van. When the Grand-Remous sites didn't pan out, they abruptly changed course. They turned south and ended up, not coincidentally, at Kingston Mills where Hamed and Shafia scouted some more.

Three days later, said Lacelle, Hamed and his father both returned to the Mills where they worked out the final details. They had already enticed Zainab home, luring her with the prospect of a wedding to Ammar Wahid. They let her take a job working at a Harvey's restaurant. By the time the three accused appeared at the Kingston Police station to report the women missing, they were all telling the same story, making sure to interject it into the interviews with police.

"Zainab took the keys to the Nissan and that's the last anyone saw of her and the three others," Lacelle described as the mantra.

But several things went badly wrong for the conspirators. They had to use the Lexus to bump the Nissan into the water after it got hung up on the side of the lock wall. Rona's diary emerged, completely authentic because it was written in 2008, when she didn't realize she would soon be dead and it would be used as evidence in a murder trial. And there were the wiretaps, not just with Shafia damning his children over and over, but with Tooba opining that while Zainab was "already done," it was too bad her two other daughters had to be killed.

During the course of the trial, there was much public speculation about whether Tooba might beat the first-degree murder charge. If the jury was going to have any similar thoughts, Lacelle worked to dispel the possibility. "She was there the moment her daughters and Rona were killed," said the attorney. Not only that, she had stayed with them and kept them calm while she waited for her husband and son to return and finish what they had plotted.

"Tooba's role was indispensable. Shafia and Hamed needed her to be part of the plan to take Rona, Zainab, Sahar, and Geeti to the locks. They needed Tooba to co-operate with them and not alert anyone to their plans," she said. "That means she was a significant contributing cause to the murders."

Lacelle went into the evening with her summation. It was a long, turbulent day for the lawyers, court staff, and the jurors. She detailed how involved Hamed was in the murder plot with his computer searches and cover-ups and evasive interviews with police. She tore apart his story about how his sisters died. "The sum total of the effort to save his sisters and Rona was to dangle a rope," she said. "Why not call 911? The truth is, he helped kill them."

Lacelle said Shafia's testimony, in which he stood by his condemnation of his daughters on the wiretaps, proved how little he valued their lives. "He said these things," she said, "in the shadows of the deaths of his daughters."

She said the Shafias had plenty of time to commit the murders. The forensic pathologist had confirmed it would only take two to three minutes to render a person unconscious by forced drowning. She asked the jury to remember the injuries to three of the women on the tops of their heads. "That's not a coincidence." Drowning the four women one by one in the basin at Kingston Mills, said Lacelle, was one possible scenario. But as jurors, they did not need conclusive evidence on that point to render guilty verdicts.

With the car hung up, needing to be pushed in, and the window down with no sign of an attempted escape by the women, Lacelle said they were "already dead or unconscious." "The evidence is overwhelming that this was not an accident. The Nissan couldn't go into the canal under its own power with the ignition off," she said. "They planned it. They deliberated on it and they carried it out together. Shafia said on the wiretap there was no other way. Find them guilty. On the evidence, there is no other way."

It was 7:07 pm when Lacelle spoke these final words. Justice Maranger dismissed the jury for the evening.

The next morning, jurors began arriving early with their packed suitcases, ready for a likely stay at an undisclosed local motel. Security again was heavy, with members of the public lined up outside the courthouse starting at 6 am to hear the judge's charge to the jury.

At 9 am, Justice Maranger started by thanking everyone involved in the case. "This was a trial with a lot of twists and turns, a lot of unexpected events," he told the jury. "No sign of complaint. It was remarkable. You did your jobs very well and I thank you for it."

It took the judge about six and a half hours to read his 250-page charge, covering all of the essential elements of the case and instructing them that they could find all three guilty of first-degree murder on four counts, or any of them could be found guilty of second- degree murder — or not guilty at all. They did not have to deliver the same verdict for each of the accused. The jury deliberated for about an hour and a half that Friday night before word came back they were stopping until the next day.

# The verdict...

JUST after 1 PM on Sunday, word got out that they had reached a decision. Events began happening at what seemed like an accelerated rate. News reporters were allowed to file into the courtroom first, followed by dozens of members of the public who somehow found out a verdict had been reached.

Just before 2 pm, Justice Maranger took his seat on the bench, followed by the jurors. The foreman handed their verdict to the court officer who relayed it to the judge.

Maranger asked the three accused to rise and he read the verdicts: Mohammad Shafia, guilty on all four counts of first-degree murder; Hamed, guilty on all four counts; Tooba, also guilty on all four counts. Hamed bent over the rail of the prisoners' box under the weight of what he'd just heard and wept; Shafia reached out to hold his son's shoulder.

The jury was polled, all verifying that they supported the verdict unanimously. One of the female jurors was crying. None of them looked as if the heavy burden they had borne for more than three months had been lifted.

The Shafias were asked if they had anything to say.

"We are not animals. We are not murderers. We did not commit murder and this is unjust," said Shafia.

"This is not just," echoed Tooba. "I am not a murderer

and I am a mother."

"Sir," Hamed told the judge, "I did not drown my sisters any-where."

Justice Maranger, however, had the verdicts in hand. "It's difficult to conceive of a more heinous, more despicable, more hon-ourless crime," he said. "The apparent reason behind these cold-blooded, shameful murders was that the four completely innocent victims offended your twisted notion of honour, a notion of honour founded upon the domination and control of women, a sick notion of honour that has no place in any civilized society." Then he sentenced each of them to life in prison with no chance for parole for 25 years.

The scene on the lawn of the Frontenac County Court House that afternoon was unlike anything Kingston had seen for many years. Dozens of Kingstonians mingled among the news reporters and camera operators and police officers to witness the conclusion of one of the most riveting legal cases in the city's history.

The Crown attorneys, Lacelle and Laarhuis, along with Detective Chris Scott, approached a bank of microphones to make a final statement. "This is a good day for Canadian justice," said Laarhuis. "It's a very sad day because this jury found that four strong, vivacious, and freedom-loving women were murdered by their own family."

One man in the crowd voiced his support for the lawyers and police: "Assistant crown attorneys Gerard Laarhuis and Laurie Lacelle did an exceptional job, their passion, their work ethic. They gave these victims a voice when they had none, so I appreciate their work," he said. The crowd applauded.

Moosa Hadi shouted his disapproval. "This is a lie. This is a miscarriage of justice," he said. Soon after, he was escorted to the edge of the courthouse property, questioned by police, and sent away.

The side doors of the limestone courthouse opened. Shafia, Tooba, and Hamed walked into the crisp winter air flanked by police officers and guards. They were led to a waiting van and whisked away.

# Honour?

THROUGH hours of video interrogation, and weeks and weeks of courtroom appearances, hearing the same allegations brought against him over and over again, Hamed Shafia did not waver. The "guilty" verdict had a different effect. His hands holding the rail of the prisoners' box, Hamed bent his head forward and his shoulders sagged. As he wept, his parents reached out to comfort him, the father, briefly, tentatively stroking the son's arm.

What had sustained the young man to this point? Even through the most damning testimony, seated in the middle of the box between his parents, he stared straight ahead, intense and seemingly dispassionate. What kept him going? A cultural belief in the righteousness of their deeds? Denial? A deep-seated belief that honour had been restored? Perhaps it was a young man's bravado — the sense that he would beat the odds.

The Crown had introduced as evidence a school assignment written by Hamed and found in his room when police raided the Montreal home in July of 2009. It barely raised an eyebrow in the courtroom at the time. But following the trial, in hindsight, it seemed more significant.

"Traditions and customs are to be followed till the end of ones [sic] life," Hamed wrote. "Actually it doesn't matter at all weather [sic] your [sic] close to the community following the specific traditions, or living millions of miles away. Tradition and customs of a person is like his identity and what makes him special even though, living in another country, surely it might feel embarrassing."

"What does honour mean to you?" a Kingston police interrogator asked Hamed after his arrest.

"It's like, uh, [if you] don't uh, tell the truth and, uh, how can you live with such a lie for the rest of your life. You can't do that," he answered. According to the 12 jurors in Kingston, Hamed, along with his parents, was living a lie of the worst kind.

There had been an estimated dozen honour killings in Canada in the decade preceding the Shafia convictions, relatively few compared to the hundreds that occur each year around the world, including the United States. Academics have seen a rise in the worldwide statistics. This may be, in part, a result of better identification of the phenomenon coupled with a willingness on the part of law officials to pursue honour as a motive for murder. As was made clear by Crown attorney Gerard Laarhuis's post-trial statements, Canadian law enforcement and justice officials want to send a clear message that such atrocities won't be tolerated here.

The Shafia murders followed similar patterns to previous cases.

## Aqsa Parvez

On a December morning in 2007, 16-year-old Aqsa Parvez was waiting at a bus stop in Mississauga, Ontario, when her brother, Waqas, 26, and her father, Muhammad, showed up and took her back to the family home. Like the Shafia girls, Aqsa rebelled against wearing traditional clothing and was given little privacy in her home. She wanted to get a part-time job and be able to go out with friends when she wanted. Twice she left home.

In an interview with police following the murder, her mother, Anwar Jan Parvez, said her husband told her he killed their daughter because "this is my insult. My community will say, You have not been able to control your daughter.' This is my insult. She is making me naked."

When police arrived, they found the girl fully clothed on her bed with blood dripping from her nose. Waqas was not at the scene. The father, who had blood on his hands, confessed to the killing, but police later determined it was the brother who had strangled his sister. His DNA was found under her fingernails, indicating she had struggled to stay alive.

In June of 2010, the father and brother were sentenced to life in prison for carrying out the honour killing. The presiding judge called Aqsa Parvez's death a "twisted and repugnant" crime carried out for the purpose "of saving family pride, for saving them from what they perceived as family embarrassment."

He characterized the case as one of abused trust and authority by the father over his daughter and hoped the life sentences would send a message of deterrence "to others that would think of committing a crime like this."

## Jassi Sidhu

Just prior to the resumption of the Shafia trial in January of 2012, another suspected honour killing case took a new turn when the mother and uncle of a woman killed in Punjab in 2000 were arrested in British Columbia.

It is alleged that 25-year-old Jassi Sidhu's family was scandalized by her secret marriage in India to a poor rickshaw driver, Mithu

Singh Sidhu. The young couple had carried on a secret long-distance relationship for four years. They married in 1999 and the following year they were ambushed in Punjab. Jassi's throat was slashed and Mithu barely survived a savage beating.

Malkit Kaur Sidhu, 63, and Surjit Singh Badesha, 67, both of Maple Ridge, B.C., were arrested under the Extradition Act after investigators in India found evidence they may have directed the attacks from Canada. Seven people had already been convicted in India for murder, attempted murder, and conspiracy to commit murder.

## Khatera Sadiqi

In Edmonton, Alberta, on the evening of September 18, 2006, Khatera Sadiqi, 20, and her fiancé Feroz Mangal, 23 went for dinner and to a movie with a group of friends that included Khatera's brother Hasibullah. At the end of the evening, Khatera and Mangal drove Hasibullah to where his car was parked. Hasibullah went to his car and pulled a loaded Smith & Wesson .44 Magnum handgun from underneath the seat. He then walked back to Khatera's car and shot the couple at close range. Khatera died instantly; Mangal died 10 days later in hospital when he was removed from life support.

During the month-long trial, witnesses said that Hasibullah Sadiqi was angered by the fact that his sister had decided to get engaged to Mangal without seeking her father's permission even though she was estranged from him. Khatera was also living with Mangal and his family, another decision that witnesses said upset Hasibullah.

In 2009, the jury found Hasibullah guilty and he was sentenced to life in prison with no chance of parole for 25 years.

## Aysar Abbas

In Ottawa in 1999, Canadian citizen Adi Abdul Humaid, originally from the United Arab Emirates, killed his 46-year-old wife Aysar Abbas by stabbing her in the neck 23 times with a steak knife, while they were visiting their son at the University of Ottawa. Humaid, who had an affair with the family maid, said he thought his wife, a successful engineer who controlled most of the family wealth, was sleeping with her business associate.

Humaid was convicted of first-degree murder and, in a bizarre turn of events, appealed to the Supreme Court of Canada to grant him a lighter sentence because he was a devout Muslim who was provoked by his wife's claim she had cheated on him, an insult so severe in the Muslim faith it deprived him of self-control.

The court refused Humaid's appeal, claiming it "is irreconcilable with the principal of gender equality" enshrined in the Charter of Rights.

## Farah Khan

In 2000, Muhammad Arsal Khan, 40, killed his five-year-old daughter Farah because he suspected she was not his biological daughter. Khan, serving a life sentence in prison, is alleged to have planned her murder before the family immigrated to Canada in the spring of 1999. He was described as a violent man who hated his daughter.

He bought surgical instruments in his native Pakistan that were then used to dismember Farah's body, which he disposed of in different locations along Toronto's waterfront.

Farah's stepmother, Kaneez Fatima, 49, was found guilty of second-degree murder because she did not do enough to stop Khan from killing the girl. Fatima's lawyer told the court that Khan had forced her to help dispose of the child's body.

Muslim leaders have been quick to condemn honour killings. They are concerned that too often their religion is associated with a practice which, they point out, is not found in any teachings in their holy book, the Koran. As the Shafia trial opened in Kingston in October of 2011, the imam at the local mosque, Sikander Hashmi, told his congregation that there is no honour in murder. "As Muslims, we have a responsibility to stand out for justice," he said.

Others are hesitant to use the term honour killing because it labels entire ethnic communities based on the actions of a few. Everyone agrees, however, that honour killings are rooted in patriarchal and tribal family systems in which the father, husband, or eldest son exerts heavy-handed control over the women.

As Shahrzad Mojab noted during her court testimony, honour killings are well-documented as a "cultural practice." When some families immigrate to other countries, they bring with them a concept from their home culture that becomes "frozen in the moment," she said.

"Globally, [it] is established that the honour killing is on the rise and has transgressed the borders of the region [in which] it has taken place and is now in the diasporas of North America and Europe as well," Mojab said.

According to Tooba's own testimony, a pact had been made with their children before they left Dubai in 2007 that they would all complete their education before taking on husbands or wives. In the meantime, there would be no dating. This was a notion that would soon clash with the children's new lives and experiences in

Canada. Claiming to be "liberal," the Shafia parents, especially Mohammad, were clearly not prepared to adapt to the secular society they were living in. He expected his daughters to behave as pious Muslims and was furious when they refused to accept the strict rules he imposed on them. As Shafia said in one of the wiretaps, if the surviving younger children were similarly disobedient, they could always move back to Dubai.

In Dubai, as in most of the Middle East, honour crimes are not treated seriously and women who report rape or sexual abuse to police are often charged with a crime themselves. Take the case of a young British Pakistani woman, celebrating her engagement to her British fiancé in Dubai. She was raped by a hotel employee and, when she reported it to police, they charged her and her fiancé with drinking alcohol and having illegal sex.

In Jordan in 1994, 16-year-old Kifaya Husayn, was tied to a chair by her 32-year-old brother. He gave her a drink of water and told her to recite an Islamic prayer. Then he cut her throat. He then ran into the street, waving the bloody knife and crying, "I have killed my sister to cleanse my honour." Kifaya's "crime" was that she was raped by another brother. Kifaya's murderer was sentenced to 15 years, but the sentence was reduced to seven-and-a-half years, an extremely severe penalty by Jordanian standards.

Middle Eastern penal codes either exempt or hand down reduced sentences to male family members who murder their female relatives. Is it any wonder women are reluctant to report crimes of abuse? And is it any wonder that people like Mohammad Shafia think they are justified in murdering their own children?

The rise of religious fundamentalism across the Arab world has contributed to limiting gender equality for women. Fundamentalists, who do not accept gender equality, imprison women within limited social and political roles. The Jordanian royal family has supported efforts to fight the practice of honour killing but, even though the religious establishment attempted to prohibit the killing of women by male family members, a conservative parliament aborted a government initiative to amend laws that were too lenient in punishing such crimes.

Middle Eastern scholars and the Islamic establishment remind us, as did Professor Shahrzad Mojab at the Shafia trial, that the concept of honour killing pre-dates religion; it is a pre-Islamic, pagan, Arab tribal ritual that has slowly and insidiously been incorporated into (predominantly Muslim) Middle Eastern and Asian culture, where, unfortunately, most honour killings occur. It is a social and cultural problem, first and foremost. It is, in fact, a problem of gender equality in a patriarchal society. The Koran does not prescribe honour killing, and prohibits the "taking of the law into one's own hands."

# The witnesses...

LATIF Hyderi has suffered greatly for his testimony at the trial. He now finds himself outside the Afghan community in Montreal, unsure sometimes whether he did the right thing when he agreed to testify against his own niece. He and his adult children have been shunned by the once close network of nine related families who emigrated from Afghanistan to Montreal. Did he do the right thing, he asks in his apartment a month after the trial ended.

"The question I ask is because, at the beginning, not just in [the] Afghan society, some of the Canadians abandoned me. We would go to the mosque and no one would talk to me," he said.

Hyderi said he and Shafia come from a culture in Afghanistan where men will kill women for honour, then go and report it to police without facing real justice. In Canada, he knew he had to stand up to Shafia. He stands by his testimony. "I request from the Afghan community, it is hard for me to see Tooba·my niece in prison. It's very shameful," he said. "No matter what they think, even if they consider me an enemy, I tell the truth and nothing else."

Fahima Vorgetts, Rona's long-distance confidante from the United States, says the Shafias were not a liberal family, despite efforts to portray themselves that way during the trial. "A liberal man would not say the devil should shit on their graves," she said, recalling the ugly wiretap rantings.

"As far as I'm concerned, the man has no honour. There is no worst dishonour than murdering somebody," she said. "I describe it as stubbornness, ignorance, lack of education — control." She believes that immigrant families need to be told when they arrive in Canada and the U.S. that "they should not be bringing their own ideas" of inequality and violent retribution.

"When people come here, they should have an education in culture and law and rights. If everyone would take a class about what are the rights here, there should be respect for that. Maybe we can save some lives."

# The lessons...

MICHELLE Dionne, a director with the Centre de jeunesse responsible for child safety in Quebec, told QMI Agency following the verdicts that inadequate investigation into the complaints relayed by the Shafia children were the result of a lack of awareness about honour killings, coupled with poor data-sharing between agencies.

Police and social workers investigated the family at home and at their school on three separate occasions. Each time the files were closed because officials said stability had been restored in the family and the children were not sticking to their complaints. Dionne said they are now more sensitive to cultural differences in suspected abuse cases.

"Our investigation did not go far [enough]," she said. "If we had had all the pieces of the puzzle at the time, it is legitimate to ask if we could have acted otherwise. The answer is yes. But, again, could we have prevented this tragedy?"

According to Melpa Kamateros, the executive director of The Shield of Athena Family Services in Montreal, an organization that helps victims of family violence, the Shafia murders are part of "a new wave of family violence" that echoes patterns from the past.

"In history, if you trace it even in European countries, you have honour crimes. The issues are, women are very often seen as objects to be controlled and to be limited and disciplined," said Kamateros.

She views honour crimes as a "sub-category" of domestic violence. "People in general are scared to label it but I think we're going in that direction. Our caseworkers are noticing situations related to honour. There are efforts to control the way a young woman dresses and the way she acts. The height of the cycle is murder," said Kamateros. "Forced marriages come into this as well."

The big difference she sees is other family members being involved in the crime. "There's family complicity," she said. "It doesn't present the same way as conjugal violence. With all this media publicity, a good thing is social services are more aware of the need to adapt. But there are still gaps to be filled."

In March of 2012, Prime Minister Stephen Harper went to the Shield of Athena Family Services to announce a grant of $348,000 for an awareness campaign against honour crimes. He specifically cited the Shafia case, saying all Canadians should remember the four women who died at Kingston. "There is nothing honourable about so-called honour crimes," said the Prime Minister. "Indeed, this is a barbaric practice which our laws rightly deem to be heinous and indefensible acts and nothing less."

The Shafias were not clients of The Shield of Athena but the organization, which offers services in 17 languages to female victims of violence, has a long history of bringing education and awareness campaigns to ethnic communities to try to stop conjugal and family violence. Melpa Kamateros said the experience of the Shafias and the Afghan community is nothing new in Canada.

"There is a historical basis to honour crimes. We're dealing with something that has been around for a long time. We can't generalize and say Afghans are violent toward their daughters. No one community is more violent than another. What we can say is people haven't benefited from the information we have had in Canada."

Kamateros agrees with Fahima Vorgetts that new immigrant families need to be given upfront a set of information, in their own language, that makes clear for them the social expectations and, particularly for women, what rights they have in their new home. "Basic information on human rights," she said. "Information on conjugal violence."

That information should include something about the history of violence, what resources are available if you are a victim of violence, the legal consequences for men, and how the family unit is damaged by family violence. That's exactly what The Shield of Athena did 20 years ago in Montreal when they realized women from Greek families who came to Canada in the 1950s wave of immigration were not showing up at shelters for women in numbers proportionate with other ethnic groups. A quick survey of 10 shelters showed that in the course of one year, only one Greek woman had come forward for protection. They translated all of the existing material into Greek and began going to Orthodox churches to speak about conjugal violence. More than 300 people would stay around after the mass to hear the talk, which was also attended by police officers and social workers.

"What we were not expecting were the victims, Kamateros recalled. "After every session we would get victims. They had lived an abusive life for the past 20 or 30 years and could not get support."

Clearly, the Shafia girls did not have a problem with communicating in French or English. They were victims of a terrible breakdown in communications between the authorities — the police and youth protection agencies — who should have been helping them.

"There's a lot of fear for women to break the cycle of violence even when they speak perfect English and French," said Kamateros. She pointed out that it is also important to get the message to the wider ethnic communities at large. "The situation is very bad for the victim but we can't give up on that community because the victim has to go back to that community."

It is clear from the reaction Latif Hyderi has received from the Afghan community in Montreal that the community is in need of information in their own language. "Our solution to that," says Kamateros, "is that you have to open that [up] even more. It's a normal reaction for the community to retract and heal their wounds. No community wants to be stigmatized as violent. Changing perceptions doesn't happen overnight but, for those with the information, they can act if they wish."

Stephen Tanner was the chief of police in Kingston from the time of the murders to the completion of the trial. "We acknowledge there is a phenomenon called honour killing," he said. "The justice system doesn't believe there is honour in killing. A murder is a murder."

Yet Tanner also recognizes that police — along with school officials and youth protection agencies — need to walk a careful line in respecting all cultures but at the same time be aware of deeper cultural issues. He believes the Shafia case involved a tragic "clash of societal values."

"We get a situation like this, which is a relatively new phenomenon, but as police we have to acknowledge it could happen again. As police leaders, we have to open our minds to be more knowledgeable of different cultures. We have to embrace those differences but learn from these more extreme cases," he said.

"At some level, we had a clashing of cultures and values. Where we live, in a free and democratic society, those same freedoms within some families or cultures may be seen as dishonourable. To some individuals, human life has less value. It's not everyone. We have to be careful not to view cultures in a biased way."

Tanner said one of the tough lessons learned in the Shafia case is that when children speak out about abuse, it is essential to allow them "to speak to us free of any outside influence." Several times, the Shafia children recanted when their parents arrived on the scene.

"We have to be increasingly aware of those sorts of things. It can be a fine balance because we're dealing with young people. We also have to know that in extreme cases, [the] parent might be where the greatest threat comes from. The provider may be the actual threat."

Rona's sister, Diba Masoomi, was asked on the witness stand why, if she had information that Rona's life was in danger, she did not report it to authorities. Diba said she tried to strengthen her sister's resolve by reminding her of where she was now living. "I told Rona, don't be afraid. This is not Afghanistan. This is not Dubai. This is Canada and you don't have any problem. Don't be afraid," she told the court.

But Rona had ample reason to be afraid in Canada. She was afraid of deportation. The two people who controlled her life by withholding her documentation and controlling her dealings with the immigration lawyer were also physically and emotionally abusive to her.

Perhaps if Latif Hyderi had received the official message that family violence was not to be tolerated and, should, in fact be reported, his actions could have been pre-emptive and not delayed until testifying after it was too late for Zainab, Sahar, Geeti and Rona.

Kamateros said she cannot comment directly on the Shafia case. But she understands the pattern. "Should we blame the community or should we point the finger at ourselves?" she asked.

# The legacy...

THE emotional damage has been deep and far-reaching. Three young men with close relationships to Zainab and Sahar lost their loves. An Afghan family and community remains divided in Montreal. Three Shafia children were left without their parents for more than three years and will have to bear a terrible legacy, their parents and eldest brother sitting in federal prisons.

Mohammad, Tooba, and Hamed have appealed their convictions.

Occasionally, a small bouquet of flowers will appear near the side of the lock at Kingston Mills where the black Nissan plunged into the waters of the Rideau Canal and four women lost their lives. They are gone but not forgotten. A women's shelter in Kingston is working to install a plaque at the lockstation to remember them. The Kingston branch of Canadians for Women in Afghanistan, which fundraises for education projects in that country, announced a special education grant created in the names of Rona, Zainab, Sahar, and Geeti.

Mary-Ann Devantro, the Shafias' neighbour on rue Bonnivet, says she walks a fine line with the surviving children. She wants to maintain contact with them — they call her or visit from time to time — but she is torn by the verdict. "It's not my place to say [their parents] did it. I'm here to support them," she said. "How would you feel if it was your mom and dad? I can't even believe the stuff I was hearing on TV."

When Diba Masoomi was in Canada to testify for her late sister Rona, Devantro met her on the street. It was unnerving. "I thought I was dreaming because she looked so much like her sister," she recalled. She keeps the earrings Rona gave her safely put away in remembrance.

Devantro saw the family leave on their trip to Niagara Falls in June of 2009. She thought it was odd that they didn't ask her to bring in the mail while they were away, as they usually did. A week later, she saw that Mohammad Shafia had returned with the van. Then detectives were all over the neighbourhood, and she knew something was terribly wrong.

She would like to move away from the memories. "If I could afford to leave, I'd leave here because the kids don't want to come around," said Devantro.

And she often thinks of the four beautiful women whose lives were taken so needlessly. "It's like they never existed," she said. "But at night I tell them, 'Be at peace.'"

(L to R) Hamed Shafia, Tooba Mohammad Yahya, and Mohammad Shafia.
Picture courtesy of Ian MacAlpine/*Kingston Whig-Standard*.